The New England Fishing Economy

THE NEW ENGLAND
FISHING ECONOMY

Jobs, Income, and Kinship

Peter B. Doeringer

Philip I. Moss

David G. Terkla

The University of Massachusetts Press

Amherst, 1986

Copyright © 1986 by The University of Massachusetts Press
All rights reserved
Printed in the United States of America
Set in Linoterm Garamond No. 3 at The University of Massachusetts Press
Printed by Cushing-Malloy and bound by John Dekker & Sons

Library of Congress Cataloging-in-Publication Data

Doeringer, Peter B.
    The New England fishing economy.

    Bibliography: p.
    Includes index.
    1. Fish trade—New England. 2. Fish trade—
Massachusetts—New Bedford. 3. Fish trade—
Massachusetts—Gloucester. 4. Fishers—Massachusetts—
New Bedford. 5. Fishers—Massachusetts—Gloucester.
6. New Bedford (Mass.)—Economic conditions.
7. Gloucester (Mass.)—Economic conditions.
I. Moss, Philip I. II. Terkla, David G. III. Title.
HD9457.A11D64   1986   338.3'7270974   86–7128
ISBN 0–87023–535–4

Contents

Acknowledgments

This book is the product of team research begun in the late spring of 1982 to determine how a shift in the United States–Canadian fishing boundary would affect socioeconomic conditions in New England. In addition to the present authors, Lauren Hasselriis-Ghom, Harry Katz, Patricia Flynn, Giulio Martini, Paul Osterman, Jay Ostrower, Michael Piore, Virginia Randall, Paul Harrington, Paul Simpson, and Michael Useem all participated in some facet of the research.

The United States State Department's "Socio-economic Task Force" headed by Jon Ollson and Raymond Meyer provided a number of constructive reviews of the initial research materials during 1982. Geoffrey Bannister, Dean of the College of Liberal Arts at Boston University and a member of the task force, kept the project moving at critical points. Glen Weisbrod of Cambridge Systematics and James Kirkley, Richard Hennemuth, and Joseph Mueller of the National Marine Fisheries Service made important unpublished data available to us.

James Kirkley read an earlier draft of this study, and William Capron, Margaret Dewar, and Susan Peterson have made helpful comments on a number of versions. Margaret Dewar, Susan Peterson, John Poggie, and Richard Pollnac allowed us to use unpublished data which they had collected from surveys of fishermen in Gloucester and New Bedford. Finally, we are grateful to a large number of people—employers, government officials, trade-union representatives, fishermen and their wives, bankers, and research specialists who gave generously of their time to help educate us in the nuances of the fishing industry.

We were pleased to be able to draw upon the special expertise of several individuals in order to develop important sections of this study. Margaret Dewar provided us with an economic review of the fishing industry in New England. Susan Peterson and Richard Pollnac prepared the chapter on the attitudes and work experience of fishermen and processing workers. Giulio Martini, Andrew Sum, and Paul Harrington assembled the economic base data and developed local multiplier estimates. These contributions provided the study with a completeness and perspective that it would have otherwise lacked.

The preparation of numerous drafts of a manuscript requires patience and tolerance as well as strong technical skills and considerable endurance. We wish to thank Fran Fox and Charlene Arzigian for being such stalwarts in this undertaking. We are also grateful to Susan Scott Gibson for coordinating the administration of the project.

This research was made possible by a grant from the William H. Donner Foundation, Inc. of New York. Additional assistance was provided by the United States Department of State and the National Oceanic and Atmospheric Administration's (NOAA) Office of Sea Grant through the Woods Hole Oceanographic Institution. None of these organizations necessarily endorses the findings of our research and we remain solely responsible for the study's shortcomings.

The New England Fishing Economy

ONE

Introduction

This is a book about the fishing industry in New England—its structure, its work force, and the way it adjusts to change. It documents the economic experience of one of America's oldest industries, one that has recently been at the center of well-publicized international boundary and trade disputes. Although the fishing industry is itself interesting, this study addresses a far larger set of issues relating to how economic institutions affect the way in which change is translated into employment and income in the economy of the United States.

At a time when significant employment declines in "mature" industries are leading to frequent calls for industrial policies to sustain employment and to facilitate adjustment to change, it is surprising how little we know about processes of labor market adjustment. It is easy to identify the major sectors of job decline from employment data; sluggishness in labor market adjustment can be detected from unemployment statistics; and the extent to which structural change ripples through the economy can be determined by using economic multipliers. With few exceptions, however, we lack comprehensive studies of how change affects specific categories of workers in particular industries.

The bulk of our knowledge about how industries adapt to structural change comes from scattered case studies conducted in the late 1950s and early 1960s.[1] These studies were motivated by a desire to understand the consequences of job loss caused by long-term declines in labor demand: industrial decline concentrated in depressed areas such as mining towns in Appalachia; the effect of textile and shoe imports on New England mill towns; and the displacement of labor through automation. Although there have been no comparable case studies in recent years, there has been a series of national statistical studies looking at unemployment, income loss, and labor market discouragement among workers displaced from jobs in declining industries.[2]

Together, these two strands of research—case studies and statistical analyses of national data—present a consistent story about adjustment difficulties. They show that labor adjustment in response to economic change is not always an easy process. Although some displaced workers become reemployed quickly, the bulk remains unemployed for as long as a year or more following layoff.[3]

Nor do the employment problems of displaced workers end for those who manage to find new jobs. National statistical studies tracking workers displaced from declining manufacturing industries, for example, find that annual losses in earnings average about 20 percent. Moreover, these pay losses are often not transitory, but persist for two years or more beyond the initial period of employment dislocation.[4]

Although the basic outlines of these adjustment difficulties are well documented, *processes* of adjustment are not. Few case studies trace through, in detail, labor market responses to structural change. Those that do, focus mainly on how workers adjust to job loss, or on how the adjustment process is managed through collective bargaining or through government programs of adjustment assistance. These case studies rarely address more fundamental questions of how matters of both efficiency and distribution are affected by the institutions of the labor market. When change occurs, do employers cut back on jobs, on pay, or on hours worked? When jobs are lost, is it the least productive, the least senior, or the least adaptable workers who face layoffs? When unions are involved, to what extent are adjustment strategies modified by collective bargaining? Do some economies respond to change more efficiently than others? To what extent do local organizations facilitate adaptation? What are the social "safety nets" that cushion change, and how do these safety nets vary among communities?

Adjustments in Small Enterprises

Most of the case studies of labor market adjustment are drawn from manufacturing and mining. As a result, they primarily involve workers in medium- and large-scale enterprises. Typically, such enterprises can be characterized as having "internal labor markets." Labor market adjustments within these internal labor markets are governed by administrative rules that are usually codified in personnel manuals and collective bargaining agreements. With few exceptions, employment levels in these enterprises fluctuate with output, and seniority is a dominant consideration in determining job security.

Because these studies focus on larger firms, they say nothing about whether firm size matters in adjusting to structural change. Do small enterprises have internal labor markets? Are there differences in adjustment processes, and in their efficiency and distributional consequences, between small and large enterprises? This study of the New England fishing industry and its labor adjustment arrangements begins to answer these questions.

The fishing industry is almost exclusively comprised of small enterprises. Apart from a handful of corporate-owned fishing vessels, most of the New England fleet is individually or family owned. Workers on these vessels never exceed fourteen and most have fewer. In addition, much of the processing and distribution of fresh fish is also conducted by small enterprises.

A close examination of the employment practices in these small enterprises reveals a rich array of adjustment procedures. Of particular interest are the kinship-based income and worksharing arrangements that are increasingly prevalent in the fish-harvesting sector. These arrangements impart a distinctly different character to adjustments in the fishing industry from those found in case studies of large-scale enterprises.

Worksharing is not unique to the fishing industry, however. It has long been a feature of the apparel and unionized construction industries, and some industrial unions have argued for worksharing as a device for meeting long-term economic decline.[5] There is also some evidence of worksharing arrangements in nonunion manufacturing in rural areas.[6] Work- and income-sharing practices are also common on family farms and in family businesses in developing countries.[7] Although work and income sharing often appear in traditional industries, some analysts have emphasized the advantages of such arrangements in modern industry as well.[8] This study provides concrete documentation of how such practices affect economic performance.[9]

Finally, there has been considerable research in recent years on the economic potential of small-scale, ethnic enterprises.[10] This study complements this research and points to a number of interesting hypotheses concerning small-business development and the role of ethnicity drawn from the experience of the New England fishing industry.

Contrasts with Other Troubled Industries

The fishing industry shares some common traits with other industries whose adjustment problems have been studied. The fishing industry work force is relatively old, poorly educated, and has few skills that are transferable to other industries. Many workers are geographically immobile because of close ties to community and family—ties that are reinforced in some ports by the presence of a large number of recent immigrants, many of whom lack facility in English. Finally, the port economies tend to have narrow industrial bases, and thus they offer limited reemployment opportunities to fishermen and processing workers.

However, the fishing industry offers some important contrasts to the other industries in which adjustments to structural change have been studied. For example, the industry has been subject to repeated economic shocks in the past two decades from unpredictable shifts in species populations, changing resource management policies, and competition from foreign vessels and imports. Most recently, the industry lost an important fishing ground as the result of a boundary dispute between the United States and Canada decided by the International Court of Justice. Unlike most studies of structural change which examine a particular instance of displacement, a study of the New England fishing industry provides a wealth of historical episodes involving adjustment to shifting economic circumstances.

Furthermore, most of the labor adjustment literature has concentrated on industries that suffer permanent, long-term declines. By comparison, the periodic shocks that contract the fishing industry are sometimes followed by growth spurts. As a result, adjustment processes in fishing frequently operate in both directions. Because both growth and decline must be accommodated, the institutions that develop for handling these adjustments in the fishing industry tend to be distinct from those in industries that suffer secular declines. As will be seen, however, adjustment processes are asymmetric. Labor is drawn into the industry much more easily than it is released.

The industry also exhibits an unusually wide variety of institutional arrangements that govern job and income security and that shape patterns of adjustment to economic change. These permit a number of comparisons among different forms of economic organization within the industry—unionized versus nonunion situations and kinship versus impersonal firms.

Importance for Fisheries Regulation

The North Atlantic fishing grounds are "common-property" resources. As such, federal and state governments have sought to regulate fishing effort to ensure that stocks are not overfished and that the fishery-based economy remains healthy. Whether the objective of fisheries management policy is to maximize society's return from the fishery, to distribute the value of the fishery equitably among different groups, or some combination of the two, knowledge about adjustment processes in the industry is crucial to the regulatory process.

Formulating sensible management policy from the point of view of economic efficiency, for example, requires knowing the costs to society of resources devoted to the fishing industry. These costs depend on the extent to which these resources can be reemployed productively outside the industry. This, in turn, hinges on which resources will leave the industry during a decline and on where and how quickly they will be reemployed.

Although there is a substantial literature on fisheries policy and regulation, much less is known about the labor market and industrial structures of the fishing industry, and about how the industry adjusts to external shocks.[11] In the absence of information on adjustment, much of this literature has assumed, explicitly or implicitly, that the movement of resources in and out of the industry is relatively easy. If it were true that adjustment is easy, efficient management would require a stricter limit on the resources devoted to fishing and on the amount of catch than if the redeployment of resources is difficult. As this book demonstrates, this assumption of flexibility is wrong.

Downward adjustment in the work force is difficult, at least for the core of the New England fishing industry. This is due partly to the labor market conditions in fishing ports, but mainly to social and institutional mechanisms that tie resources to the industry. As a result, resources often remain idle during bad times rather than being reemployed outside the industry.

Moreover, rigidities in the adjustment process are not uniformly spread throughout the industry. There are many competing segments within the industry—large versus small vessels, kinship versus union boats, and among ports—and several different "margins" along which adjustment can occur. Depending upon the regulatory regime adopted, the economic position of various groups will be affected differentially at each of these margins. By identifying these different groups and their adjustment behavior, this study helps to predict the distributional consequences of regulatory actions and also helps to explain the sources of political pressure on the regulatory system.

Considerations such as these lead us to question some of the economic and organizational assumptions that have guided United States regulatory policy since the enactment of the 200-mile fishing limit in 1976. Our findings about the ease of resource entry and the difficulty of exit, for example, make the case for more liberal catch allowances than would be dictated by traditional calculations of maximum economic yield based upon the assumption of high labor mobility. The findings relating to the distributional effects of regulatory policy carry implications for the criteria to be used in selecting industry and community representation on regulatory advisory committees and for the types of economic information that should be used in reaching regulatory decisions.

The Importance of Economic Structure and the Economic Environment

Although much of the process of adjustment to economic change is determined by institutional arrangements within the industry, the facility with which labor resources released from the industry can be redeployed also depends on the characteristics of the industry's labor force and the alternative employment opportunities available. This study presents new data on the skills, industry attachment, and economic options of fishermen and processing workers in the key fishing ports in New England.

It shows how kinship, ethnicity, attitudes toward fishing as an occupation, and economic institutions all contribute to adjustment rigidities and to idle resources during downturns in the industry. Because the bulk of the New England fishing industry is concentrated in economically fragile ports, the study also explores the job prospects of displaced fishermen and the broader effects of the fishing industry on port economies.

These findings further reinforce the conclusion that resource management policies must reflect adjustment processes. They also indicate the importance of taking local conditions into account when looking at the distributive consequences of regulatory policy. Both considerations argue for a special policy focus on local economic development in conjunction with more typical fisheries policies.

Design of the Study

In addition to providing an in-depth analysis of how income and employment in the fishing industry are affected by economic change, and how such change relates to the larger structure of port economies, this book demonstrates the usefulness of an unconventional research methodology. The study blends the analysis of customary sources of economic data with field interviews, original survey data, and analyses of economic institutions.

Much of the data for the study is derived from extensive field interviews conducted in the late 1970s and early 1980s with fishermen, boat owners, and processors. These interviews were supplemented by others with many large employers and small businessmen in Gloucester and New Bedford in 1982 and 1983. In addition, we consulted widely with local officials concerned with economic development; with government agencies responsible for fisheries management; with officials from the Massachusetts Division of Employment Security and employment and training specialists in both communities; with officials of trade unions that represent fishermen, dock workers, and processing workers; with fishermen's wives; and with a variety of research experts on fishing and processing. Through these interviews and survey materials, we were able to check and crosscheck our findings to provide a reliable portrayal of the fishing industry, the local economies involved, and the linkages between fishing and the local economies.

The case-study approach has allowed us to obtain detailed information on the attitudes of workers in the industry; on the characteristics of workers placed "at risk" by economic change in fishing; and on alternative employment opportunities in specific ports. We have also been able to document the adjustment strategies adopted by fishing vessels and processing plants and the policy strategies developed by local governments to cope with economic disruption.

This study has also led to new models of labor market behavior and improved predictions about the consequences of economic change at the local level. For example, we are able to distinguish between the consequences of *marginal* economic changes in the fishing industry, for which there is considerable statistical data, and more substantial changes, for which there is far less information. We can also determine which workers are likely to lose their jobs, whose income will be affected, the reemployment prospects for dislocated workers, and the economic consequences for fishing ports from a decline in the fishing industry. The result is a set of findings that are at the level of detail essential to sound policy making at the local level.

THE CASE STUDIES

We concentrate our analysis of the New England fishing industry on the ports of Gloucester and New Bedford in Massachusetts. These two ports account for almost two-thirds of the tonnage of groundfish processed annually in New England and for over half of the annual value of total New England landings of all species. Fishing and processing are key industries in both communities, accounting for 19 percent of the jobs in Gloucester and for 7 percent of those in the New Bedford area. Multiplier estimates indicate that at least an equivalent number of additional jobs in these communities result from the income generated by the fishing industry. [12]

Fishing and processing in these two ports are also sufficiently distinct to provide useful comparisons. The ports differ in size and species caught. There are also sharp contrasts in the economic structure and overall prosperity of the two ports. The Gloucester economy is much more narrowly specialized in activities such as fishing, fish processing, and tourism. Gloucester, however, has been somewhat less vulnerable to recessions than New Bedford because of new growth in manufacturing.

Gloucester and New Bedford are also the principal offshore fishing ports in New England. The offshore industry is the economically dominant sector of the industry—accounting for over 80 percent of the value of the total New England catch and representing the core of large vessels and of fishermen committed to full-time employment. [13]

The offshore industry has also been at the center of recent policy disputes. Since 1976 it has been the subject of federal regulatory policy. It is more vulnerable to foreign competition than the inshore industry and the primary offshore fishing ground, Georges Bank, has been the site of a continuing boundary dispute between the United States and Canada. Now that the United States has lost some rights to fish on Georges Bank,

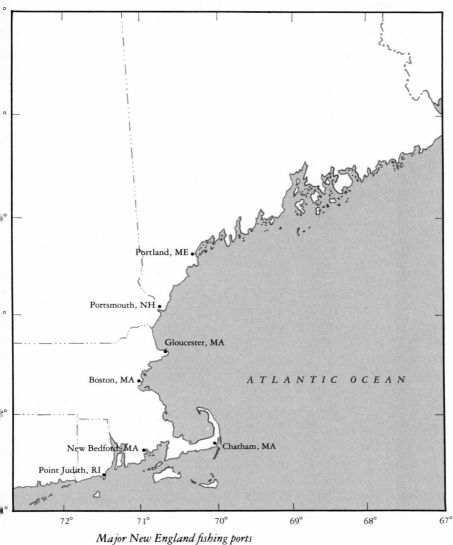

Portland, ME •

Portsmouth, NH •

Gloucester, MA •

Boston, MA •

ATLANTIC OCEAN

New Bedford, MA •   • Chatham, MA

Point Judith, RI •

72°   71°   70°   69°   68°   67°

Major New England fishing ports

substantial changes in current fishing practices in New Bedford and Gloucester are likely and the offshore industry will probably be at an increased disadvantage in competition with Canada.

Plan of the Book

The book is divided into two parts. Part 1 develops background materials on the industry, its work force, and the local port economies. Chapter 2 presents an overview of the changes in the fishing industry in New England since 1960. It outlines the principal influences upon income and employment in the New England fishing industry and discusses the major policy issues affecting the industry.

Chapter 3 describes the economic trends and economic and institutional setting of fishing and fish processing in Gloucester and New Bedford. Particular emphasis is placed upon income and employment in fishing and the growing significance of Italians and Portuguese in the fishing industry.

Chapter 4 examines the social and cultural dimensions of the labor force in fishing and processing in the two ports. It discusses the role of ethnicity and kinship in these sectors, the nature of job skills, and the attitudes of workers toward their jobs.

Part 2 addresses the dynamics of adjustment to economic change. Chapter 5 examines adjustments in employment and income within the fishing industry in response to economic change. It describes the institutional rules governing employment and pay in different parts of the fishing industry and demonstrates how these rules operate to determine the incidence of change within the industry.

In chapter 6, the wider question of employment flows between fishing and the rest of the economy is explored. The extent of skill transferability, the comparability of earnings, and the income and employment alternatives for displaced fishermen and processing workers are assessed.

The final chapter presents the conclusions of the study. It develops a series of innovative recommendations for fisheries management policies, based upon a recognition of rigidities in labor adjustment, and addresses policies for facilitating economic adjustment and promoting stabilization and growth in port economies. It also addresses more general questions of adjustments to structural change within small enterprises.

PART ONE

The Industry and the Labor Force

TWO

New England's Fishing Industry

The fishing industry in New England stretches back to colonial times. Although the industry has always experienced year-to-year fluctuations in catch, in the past two decades its fortunes have been particularly unsettled by intense foreign competition for resources and by changing policies toward fisheries management. This chapter examines the recent history of the industry to show how the economic and policy climates have changed and to provide background for the detailed study of the industry's two key ports, Gloucester and New Bedford.

The Last Two Decades

Fishermen landed over 318,000 metric tons of fish and shellfish in New England ports in 1965 and almost the same amount—312,000 metric tons—in 1982 (see table 2-1). This similarity in catch, however, masks large changes in the industry, particularly in income and employment.

In 1965 the value of the catch stood at $75 million. In 1982 fishermen and boat owners received almost five times that amount, $374 million. As a point of reference, gross national product grew 4 1/2 times during this period. The growth in income generated an expansion in the numbers of vessels and jobs. In 1965 nearly 4,000 fishermen worked on about 700 vessels over five gross tons, but by 1979, well over 5,000 fishermen worked on more than 1,300 such vessels. In 1965 about 5,400 fishermen had worked full time on very small boats under five gross tons; by 1979 that number had more than doubled and the small-boat fleet included over 21,000 vessels.

Growth in revenues and employment, however, has been extremely uneven. Fishermen, boat owners, and processors have gone through periods when they could not cover costs and have experienced other times

This chapter was written by Margaret E. Dewar.

TABLE 2–1   Weight and Value of New England Landings, 1965–1982

	Fish		Shellfish and Other		Total	
	Metric tons	Value (in millions)	Metric tons	Value (in millions)	Metric tons	Value (in millions)
1965	291,236	$ 39	27,271	$ 36	318,507	$ 75
1966	282,809	43	27,621	35	310,430	78
1967	257,277	35	26,376	35	283,652	70
1968	254,437	35	33,483	41	287,920	76
1969	219,139	36	38,625	44	257,264	81
1970	204,600	40	36,383	51	240,983	91
1971	196,666	39	36,266	56	232,932	95
1972	186,705	45	35,218	62	221,923	107
1973	202,022	52	33,008	65	235,030	117
1974	203,783	56	33,217	68	237,001	124
1975	193,547	71	32,509	83	226,056	154
1976	213,847	81	34,489	93	248,336	174
1977	228,409	95	37,383	112	265,792	207
1978	263,860	125	35,840	132	299,699	256
1979	280,489	144	40,932	158	321,422	302
1980	318,153	154	39,321	173	357,475	327
1981	273,392	157	42,764	198	316,156	356
1982	266,348	178	45,429	196	311,777	374

SOURCES: U.S. Department of Commerce, National Marine Fisheries Service, *Fishery Statistics of the United States, 1965–1977*, and *Fisheries of the United States, 1978–1982;* Unpublished data, National Marine Fisheries Service, 1978–1982.

when they made more money than most of them had earned before. They experienced moderate slumps and periods of modest prosperity as well. Various species of fish have fluctuated between abundance and near depletion. The boom-and-bust character of the industry has meant that fishermen, boat owners, owners of processing plants, and processing workers have faced frequent, and often large, fluctuations in employment and incomes. As a result, those in the fishing industry have had to adjust often to new economic conditions.

Fluctuations in catch, revenues, and jobs have been influenced by a variety of factors. The public's demand for fish, which affects price and therefore revenues, has increased because of altered attitudes and tastes. Changes in the technology of boats, in addition to changes in the volume of catch, have affected the number of fishing jobs. The size and composition of the harvest has varied because of biological factors and fisheries management policies. The most prominent factor affecting catch in New England during the 1970s, however, was the intense competition from

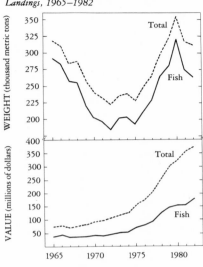

FIGURE 2–1   *Weight and Value of New England Landings, 1965–1982*

SOURCES: See Table 2–1.

foreign fishing fleets and the subsequent removal of these fleets by legislation passed in 1976.

The Effects of Foreign Competition, 1965–1976

New England and Canadian offshore fishermen traditionally had the rich grounds off the New England coast virtually to themselves, but that changed in the 1960s. Modern Russian vessels arrived to fish on Georges Bank, New England's principal offshore grounds, for the first time in 1960. In the following years, hundreds more Russian vessels and many boats from other countries came to fish the New England waters. In 1960 United States fishermen landed almost 90 percent of the fish harvested from Georges Bank and all the fish caught off southern New England. Canadian fishermen harvested most of the remaining 10 percent. By 1972 American fishermen caught only a little over 10 percent of the harvest from Georges Bank and about 12 percent of the harvest from southern New England.[1]

As the New England fleet's share of the total catch fell, the volume of the landings also declined (see table 2-1 and fig. 2-1). From a total of over 318,000 metric tons in 1965, which was the first year foreign catches

TABLE 2–2   Numbers of New England Fishermen and Boats, 1965–1979

| | | Fishermen | | | Boats | |
| | | On boats* and shore | | | Boats* | |
	On vessels*	Full time	Part time	Vessels*	Motor	Other
1965	3,952	5,399	10,084	703	10,412	405
1966	3,874	5,057	9,587	704	9,555	344
1967	3,847	4,919	9,277	714	9,294	354
1968	3,689	5,164	9,327	695	9,429	297
1969	3,537	5,501	10,911	695	10,549	251
1970	3,236	6,885	12,097	686	11,703	252
1971	3,202	7,465	12,095	699	11,535	172
1972	3,233	8,791	13,235	687	12,528	249
1973	3,035	9,252	14,638	692	13,246	233
1974	3,084	7,908	18,419	731	14,412	191
1975	3,231	9,562	18,892	770	15,499	269
1976	3,576	9,783	17,115	855	15,285	307
1977	3,893	9,885	17,964	929	15,221	230
1978**	4,183	9,908	18,455	1,024	16,433	177
1979**	5,360	——	——	1,339	——	——

SOURCE: U.S. Department of Commerce, National Marine Fisheries Service, *Fishery Statistics of the United States*, 1965–1977; National Marine Fisheries Service, unpublished data, 1978–1979.

*Vessels are 5 gross tons and over. Boats are less than 5 gross tons.

**Preliminary figures, as of December 1985.

from New England offshore fishing grounds exceeded those of the United States and Canada, New England landings of fish and shellfish fell by about one third by 1972, then increased slightly by the time Congress passed legislation to restrict foreign fishing in 1976.[2]

Revenues rose from $75 million in 1965 to $107 million in 1972, an average increase of slightly over 5 percent per year in nominal dollars compared to an average annual increase of about 8 percent in nominal gross national product in the same period. By 1976, however, the story was different. The value of fish and shellfish landings increased to $174 million, a 63 percent increase since 1972, compared to only a 45 percent increase in gross national product over the same period.[3]

Although the overall trends show the general direction of fortunes in the industry, they do not necessarily reflect the experiences of particular groups of workers, and they mask important differences among various sectors of the industry. Fishermen harvest different species, sell their catch in different markets, and work out of different ports. In contrast to the flexibility of the inshore fleet made up of small boats (generally under

60 gross tons), the large-vessel, offshore sector is more rigid. Few off-shore fishermen switch from one major type of fishing to another, move to another port, convert their boats to use gear suited for harvesting other species, or abandon fishing for other types of work. Therefore, changes in the demand for and in the abundance of fish of different species affect groups of fishermen differently.

For example, foreign fishing pressures affected fisheries such as haddock, cod, and flounder. In contrast, scalloping, also a predominately offshore fishery, felt the effects very little because foreign vessels were prohibited from fishing for scallops. However, the scallop fishery was substantially affected by shifting availability of stocks. The inshore industry also had varied experiences.

THE OFFSHORE GROUNDFISH INDUSTRY

The offshore groundfish industry is made up of vessels that work the offshore fishing areas to harvest bottom-feeding fish—cod, haddock, ocean perch, pollock, flounders, and species caught primarily as bycatch (cusk and white hake). Most of the offshore groundfish fleet originally worked out of Gloucester and Boston, Massachusetts, with a few additional vessels landing their catch in Portland and Rockland, Maine. By the mid-1960s, New Bedford, Massachusetts, had become a major port specializing in flounders and scallops and Boston had declined substantially (although it remained a major marketing center).

Landings from the offshore fleet declined sharply through the 1960s and early 1970s and then fluctuated between 61,300 and 62,800 metric tons from 1972 through 1976.[4] The most drastic decline came in haddock landings. In 1965, New England vessels landed nearly 60,800 metric tons of haddock, but this had fallen to about 3,700 metric tons by 1974. Landings per day fished, an indicator of the condition of the haddock stock, fell from 5.6 metric tons in 1965 to 2.8 metric tons by 1969.

As depletion of haddock became a "crisis" in the view of government and industry spokesmen, groundfish boats turned more effort toward harvesting cod. New England cod landings rose from over 16,000 metric tons in 1965 to more than 25,000 metric tons in 1976 as a result of more intensive fishing, although total catch (including foreign vessels) from the New England offshore grounds decreased after the mid-1960s as the stock became depleted.[5]

Yellowtail flounder, a mainstay of the New Bedford finfishing fleet, was also heavily depleted by foreign fishing in the late 1960s and early

1970s. New England landings of yellowtail flounder fell by more than half, from 34,700 metric tons in 1965 to about 17,000 metric tons in 1976.[6] This depletion of the flounder stock sent fishermen in search of cod, and even haddock, despite their lower value and haddock's scarcity.

The decline in the stocks greatly alarmed the New England offshore groundfishermen. As one Gloucester fisherman said, "There will be no fish and with no fish there will be no boats and no fish plants." In the view of another, "Years ago we used to get capacity loads, now all we are doing is scraping the bottom. The industry as a whole has declined to a disaster point."[7]

Even as they and many others described very gloomy conditions and an even worse future, incomes were improving in the offshore fleet. Almost no one talked about the new prosperity, but by the mid-1970s real income in the offshore groundfishery was greater than at any time since World War II. By 1974 a crewman on a Gloucester offshore boat earned $15,000 to $20,000 per year. In 1975 one retired Gloucester skipper who had spent thirty-five years at sea and who came from a prominent Gloucester fishing family called reports of hard times in the fishing industry "all hogwash." On the vessel his son skippered, crew members earned $15,000 in 1973 and a little more in 1974. Cooks, engineers, and skippers, who earned additional shares of the vessel revenues, could make between $18,000 and $20,000 for ten or eleven months of work. By comparison, full-time earnings averaged $11,000 in manufacturing and $8,000 in services in 1974.[8]

By 1976, when Congress passed legislation to prohibit most foreign fishing within 200 miles of the New England coast, conditions were even better for the offshore groundfish industry. The average gross return for an otter trawl vessel, the type that harvested groundfish, increased by more than 30 percent between 1974 and 1976, well ahead of growth and inflation in the rest of the economy.[9]

Several factors affected the incomes of fishermen. Declining supplies of fish and a growing consumer demand contributed to rising prices, which in turn raised fishing revenues. In addition, the number of fishermen declined as the new technology of stern trawling made boat operation possible with fewer crew than had been required by older side-trawling methods. Lower catches per fishing day also meant that fewer men were needed to clean and pack the fish. The incomes of the fewer fishermen who remained increased greatly as demand grew.[10]

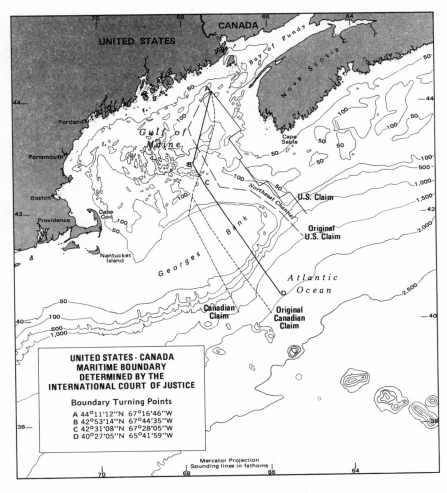

*United States–Canada Maritime Boundary, determined
by the International Court of Justice*

The processors and wholesalers who bought groundfish at the dock had similar experiences—that is, the quantity of fish they handled declined, and their revenues grew slowly in the 1960s and early 1970s, but improved in the mid-1970s. Their fortunes were linked to those of offshore groundfish boat owners and fishermen, but the processors and dealers handled a wider range of species than the groundfish vessels landed. This flexibility gave them some resilience when levels of catch declined.

The dealers in Boston who bought groundfish from offshore vessels diversified into other species by the 1960s and 1970s, although groundfish was still the primary product. They also handled more fish from Gloucester, New Bedford, Canada, and small ports in Massachusetts and Maine. The dealers in Gloucester who bought groundfish also handled the diverse landings of inshore boats. In New Bedford, buyers who primarily handled yellowtail flounder began buying groundfish as fishermen harvested more of them in the 1970s.

THE OFFSHORE SCALLOP INDUSTRY

The experiences of fishermen, boat owners, and processors in the offshore scallop industry were very different because the non-Canadian foreign fleets' intense fishing did not directly affect offshore scallopers. In addition, the industry had been healthier than the offshore groundfishery since World War II. Only Canadian and American vessels exploited the Georges Bank scallop resource. The ups and downs faced by New England scallopers were primarily generated by shifting resource conditions in various grounds and by increased competition from the Canadian fleet.

In 1965 New England scallop fishermen brought in 5,600 metric tons of scallops. Nearly all the offshore scallop fleet worked out of New Bedford. During the mid- to late-1960s more than 95 percent of the scallops landed in New England came into New Bedford, and small inshore boats landed the rest.[11]

Catches declined through the 1960s and the 1970s. After 1965, as Georges Bank beds became depleted, New Bedford vessels fished most heavily on more productive grounds off the mid-Atlantic states, but by the early 1970s the mid-Atlantic beds were also depleted. Landings fell to around 1,800 metric tons in 1973, one-third the level of 1965. By 1975, however, catches from the mid-Atlantic grounds improved; landings rose 80 percent over 1973 levels to over 3,200 metric tons, and in 1976 landings of scallops increased even more—to over 5,400 metric tons—because of the discovery of new beds off Chatham, Massachusetts.[12]

Unlike the situation in the offshore groundfish industry in the 1960s, incomes in offshore scalloping were high. In 1967 a crew share on a New Bedford scallop vessel paid about $9,300 and a captain's share about $16,400. By 1968, a crewman's share rose to more than $12,000 and a captain's share to nearly $21,000. These earnings compared very favorably with the average for a full-time manufacturing worker, nearly $6,900 in 1967 and about $7,350 in 1968. The owner's payment, net of operating costs, on a New Bedford vessel was nearly $7,100 before depreciation and income taxes in 1967 and close to $15,000 in 1968. Although income data are not available for later years, the average annual gross receipts, or "gross stock," for a sample of offshore scallop vessels suggest that incomes were high even though two major costs, food and fuel, rose considerably. Average gross receipts of a sample of offshore scallopers over 125 gross tons rose at an annual rate of nearly 19 percent, from $243,000 in 1970 to $683,000 in 1976. The receipts of a sample of vessels between 61 and 125 gross tons grew nearly 18 percent per year from $275,000 in 1970 to $732,000 in 1976, compared to slightly over 9 percent annual growth in the rest of the economy.[13]

Although these gross receipts must have translated into relatively high incomes, the number of vessels dredging for scallops fell from about sixty in 1965 to about forty-five in 1970 and stayed around forty-five through 1975. During the 1960s and early 1970s many owners of scallopers converted their vessels from dredging to otter trawling so that they could fish for yellowtail flounder. Of a group of forty-three offshore vessels dredging for scallops out of New Bedford in 1965, thirteen had converted to otter trawling by 1971.

Some boat owners took their vessels to other ports. In the most dramatic move, four large New Bedford scallopers departed in 1968 for a new scallop fishery in Alaska. Scalloping in New Bedford did not have a future, the boat owners said. They were not certain that prices would improve, too many boats were fishing, and scallops were becoming scarce. They complained that two buyers could control the price of scallops at the dock.

Fishermen and boat owners often blamed imports from Canada for the lower prices and incomes in 1973 and 1974. They sought duties on scallops through the Tariff Commission, even though imports of scallops fell below their 1972 level in 1973 and 1974.

Landed scallop prices were also depressed by rising costs of handling and processing in 1973 and 1974 and by a doubling of margins for scallops. Prices fishermen received might have fallen even more, but other conditions counteracted the effects of rising handling and processing costs. Depletion of the scallop beds reduced supply, and consumer demand grew due to higher prices for meat and fish, changing tastes, and, in 1973, rising incomes.[14]

In 1975, when the mid-Atlantic beds became more productive again, incomes improved greatly. The gross receipts of a sample of medium-sized New England scallopers jumped by nearly 50 percent in 1975 and rose nearly 35 percent more by 1976. For larger vessels over 125 gross tons, receipts rose more than 70 percent from 1974 to 1975 and by more than 30 percent between 1975 and 1976. The number of scallop dredges, including inshore boats, nearly doubled between 1975 and 1976 in response to the high incomes. Because smaller inshore boats could reach the Chatham beds to take advantage of the "bonanza," as fishermen termed the money to be made from the plentiful scallops, the share of landings and revenues attributable to the offshore fleet fell.[15]

The fortunes of the processing and wholesaling firms that handled sea scallops were largely independent of those of fishermen and boat owners, primarily because the seafood dealers depended on other species for most of their income. In 1970 and 1971 scallops accounted for 50 to 70 percent of the value of fish and shellfish handled by the two major dealers, but contributed a much smaller percentage of their profits. Processing firms that bought scallops from the wholesalers had diverse product lines and also purchased scallops from Canada, so they did not depend significantly on New England scallop landings.[16]

THE INSHORE FISHERIES

Because the inshore fleet consists of boats that cannot make long trips and cannot work in bad weather, fishermen have to choose species they can harvest from close to shore. Which species they pursue depends on fish migration, abundance, and prices, and on their preferences for different kinds of work. Unlike the offshore fishermen, inshore fishermen's livelihoods depend on their ability to be flexible as stock abundance and prices change. Despite their flexibility, they are affected by biological and economic changes in certain fisheries because differences in fish migration and abundance along the coast limit them to certain fisheries.[17]

Indeed, along most of the New England coast, inshore fishermen depended on groundfish for part of their income and were concerned about the poor condition of the stocks. The spokesman for Associated Fisheries of Maine, an organization of fish dealers and processors, stated that small-scale fishermen could no longer be certain enough of the future to invest in new boats, and the president of the Maine Fishermen's Co-op Association claimed that depletion and the scattering of schools of fish meant that inshore fishermen could not meet expenses in dragging for groundfish.[18] Only the ability to work in other fisheries and at other jobs sustained the incomes of these fishermen.

Fish dealers, including cooperatives, and processors in the many small ports where inshore fishermen landed their catch were usually as diversified as the fishermen because they bought everything the boats brought in. Therefore, their incomes changed as fishermen's did.

In summary, from 1965 through 1976 the New England fishing industry faced considerable change. The offshore industry felt the changes most acutely. Intense foreign fishing badly depleted the groundfish stocks and caused American catches to fall. Heavy American and Canadian fishing depleted the offshore scallop beds. Although catch declined and returns were very low in the groundfishery until the early 1970s, the number of vessels in the offshore industry stayed about the same. Fishing employment fell as changes in the technology of finfishing and the decline in catch meant fewer fishermen were needed to handle the harvest. As catch declined and demand for fish increased, prices rose. In scalloping, fishermen's incomes were always attractive, but their earnings revived substantially in the groundfishery, too, by the mid-1970s as a result of rising prices and the decline in the number of fishermen. As incomes rose, additional vessels and fishermen entered the industry.

The flexibility of inshore fishermen helped insulate them from the effects of foreign fishing, just as it sheltered them from other influences such as their own overfishing of inshore species or pollution that reduced certain species and eliminated some fishing areas. Although groundfish stocks on which they depended became depleted, they were able to move to other fisheries or to jobs on shore. The inshore fishery tended to respond readily to economic changes in the industry. Boats and employment declined in the late 1960s, and showed growth through the mid-1970s.

Relief from Foreign Competition

Although landings had improved slightly and incomes were high during the early 1970s, boat owners, fishermen, and processors continued to press Congress for legislation to prohibit foreigners from fishing near the coast. Getting rid of foreigners, they believed, would solve depletion problems in the groundfishery. In 1976 Congress passed the Fishery Conservation and Management Act which excluded foreigners from fishing grounds within 200 miles of the United States coast except under special conditions. As fishermen, boat owners, and dealers waited for the 200-mile limit to go into effect in March 1977, they believed they could only benefit if "the Russians" left. Contrary to the picture of financial trouble presented in the press and generally encouraged by those in the industry, most were enjoying incomes higher than at any time since World War II. Many were sure the 200-mile limit could bring even better times.

THE BOOM OF THE LATE 1970S

As the law went into effect, the industry's prosperity surpassed any of the cautious hopes fishermen, boat owners, and processors voiced publicly. In 1977 groundfish landings rose 21,000 metric tons above the harvest of 1976, an increase of approximately 34 percent. Fishermen reported that groundfish were schooling again and therefore were easier to locate and catch. Revenues rose almost as much as the harvest, from $29 million to nearly $38 million, an increase of nearly 30 percent. The average crew share on an offshore trawler that displaced between 50 and 125 gross tons rose 7 percent. On a trawler over 125 gross tons, an average crew share grew 25 percent. A crewman could earn $25,000 in a year on an offshore boat, about twice the earnings a manufacturing worker could expect.[19]

Coincidentally, the offshore scallop industry rebounded also, as landings rose to over 8,100 metric tons, an increase of 50 percent above the 1976 landings, and revenues rose to nearly $30 million. Fishermen on scallopers could earn even more than groundfish crewmen, about $30,000. These earnings were more than twice the average for a manufacturing worker, nearly three times the average for a worker in the service industries.[20]

Although inshore fishermen did not earn as much as fishermen on offshore vessels, they also prospered as fish prices continued to rise. In 1977 fishermen who owned their boats in Chatham, Massachusetts, reported personal incomes that averaged between $15,000 and $20,000. Out of a group of seventeen boat owners, seven had incomes over $20,000. Crewmen earned less, between $10,000 and $15,000.[21]

In response to the prosperity, many offshore skippers and families in offshore fishing decided to purchase new vessels. Outside investors decided to go into offshore fishing with new boats. Even larger numbers of inshore fishermen bought new boats, and newcomers to inshore fishing decided to purchase their first small boats.

State and local government officials looked for ways to make public investments to capture more of the growth of employment and income in fishing for their jurisdictions. Portland, Boston, and Gloucester received federal money for harbor development that included pier expansion and renovation. Chatham, Woods Hole, Nantucket, and other small communities considered or began smaller-scale pier and harbor improvements.[22]

THE DECLINE IN FISHING PROSPERITY

The boom was short lived. This was in part the result of the implementation of the Fishery Conservation and Management Act which instituted quotas on the catch for given periods of time. In part it was due to large increases in fuel costs and interest rates. Most of all, the bust was caused by the rapid entry of boats into the industry in anticipation of sustained prosperity. As overfishing continued, the stocks remained severely depleted, and each boat's fishing costs stayed high.

By the fall of 1977, those in the fishing industry began to realize that the Fishery Conservation and Management Act did more than get rid of foreigners, and that they would not be left alone to enjoy the boom. The law also set up fishery management councils of industry representatives and government officials to regulate the use of the fish resources in the fishery conservation zone.[23] As the 200-mile limit went into effect, the New England Fishery Management Council set quotas for the total catch to prevent further depletion of the haddock, cod, and yellowtail flounder stocks.[24] By September 1977, only six months after the law went into effect, fishermen had caught so many fish that they were forbidden under the fishery management plan to harvest more than a small amount per trip. When the catch restrictions failed to keep the harvest of fish under the levels the fishery management plan had prescribed, the director of the National Marine Fisheries Service "closed" the fishery so that fishermen could not legally land any haddock, cod, or yellowtail flounder.[25]

By prescribing the amount of fish that could be harvested in a given period of time, the quota system encouraged fishermen to catch fish as fast as possible in order to get their share before others did. In addition, as the fishing boom attracted new boats and fishermen into the industry, the larger number of boats caught the quotas even faster. When they exhausted the quota and faced restrictions, fishermen protested the financial hardships imposed by the regulations.[26] Their protests persuaded the fishery management council and Washington officials to increase the quotas. As a result, the total catch rose far above the original "optimum yield," the estimate of the "maximum sustainable yield . . . modified by any relevant economic, social, or ecological factor."[27]

Even if the council and the secretary of commerce had not raised optimum yield, fishermen would have overfished the resources because the National Marine Fisheries Service could not enforce the management measures. Fishermen learned quickly that they could land more fish than the regulations allowed without being caught and found loopholes in the regulations that allowed them to catch more than the council had presumably intended.

Fishery management not only failed to stabilize or restore the fish stocks, it also failed to achieve the other major goal of the legislation, to assure the prosperity of the industry. The law offered the possibility that fishery management could temper the industry's booms and busts and provide stable incomes over long periods. Landings of groundfish rose to almost 114,800 metric tons in 1980, an increase of approximately 85 percent over landings in 1976, but declined to about 98,400 metric tons by 1982. Revenues multiplied 2 1/2 times, growing from about $29 million in 1976 to $75 million in 1982. Despite the growth, incomes in the offshore groundfish industry began to fall. The average crew share on an offshore groundfish vessel between 50 and 125 gross tons rose to 21 percent above the 1976 level in 1978, but by 1980 was back at the 1976 level. In 1980, in real dollars, a crew share paid less than 75 percent of a crew share in 1976. In 1980, on vessels over 125 gross tons, the average crew share was 19 percent above the 1976 level, but in real dollars a crew share brought less than 90 percent of earnings in 1976.[28]

The fall in incomes meant that when prices were low, boat owners could not cover their costs. In spring and summer 1980 groundfish prices fell, as they did every year when landings rose and the weather allowed boats to spend more time fishing. The decline put many boat owners and fishermen in serious difficulty. "How are we supposed to maintain our homes and families on $100 for nine days of fishing?" asked a Gloucester fisherman's wife. New Bedford fishermen voted not to work until prices rose. Again in spring 1981, the fall in prices caused severe problems. "If this keeps up," said one Gloucester skipper, "you'll see a lot of boats tie up. I don't see any way for them to make it."[29]

One reason that incomes fell as total revenues rose was that so many additional boats now harvested groundfish. In addition to substantial increases in the inshore fleet, the offshore fleet had also begun to expand. The number of offshore groundfish vessels between 61 and 125 gross tons increased 75 percent between 1976 and 1979. The number of larger vessels, over 125 gross tons, increased 144 percent. By 1979, 430 offshore vessels landed cod, haddock, and yellowtail flounder in New England, whereas in 1976, only 256 had done so. Because boats ordered earlier continued to arrive and because few owners were able or wished to leave the industry, this offshore growth did not reverse as incomes deteriorated, and the number of boats did not stabilize until 1981. Nineteen eighty-one was a bad year, said a processing-plant manager who had served on the fishery management council, because more boats were trying to harvest from a fish stock that had grown little if at all. "It's just like a pie that's cut into 400 pieces," he said of the management quotas. "You cut it into 800 pieces, and the pie hasn't grown; everybody's just getting a smaller piece."[30]

Another closely related reason for falling incomes was that costs of fishing increased, leaving a smaller amount of a boat's revenues for distribution to fishermen as wages and to skipper-owners as wages and returns to capital. Boat owners who had paid $2,000 per trip for diesel fuel for a large trawler in 1978 had to pay at least $5,000 per trip in the winter of 1981. In addition, owners of the new offshore trawlers that had come into the groundfish industry in the first few years after the 200-mile limit went into effect had to meet much higher mortgage payments due to both larger principals and higher interest rates. Older vessels might have no mortgages at all, as boat mortgages are usually for a ten-year term.[31]

The nationwide recession also hurt. In late 1981 fresh-fish processors reported sales declines. As processors had trouble selling fish, they paid the fishermen lower prices.

THE DECLINE IN OFFSHORE
SCALLOPING PROSPERITY

The experience of the offshore scallop industry in the first years under fishery management showed no more promise than that of the groundfish industry. The fishery management council began to work on a plan for the scallop industry in 1978, and the plan was implemented in 1982. The principal management measure controlled the number of scallop meats allowed per pound.[32]

The fishery management plan for offshore scalloping had not been in place long enough to offer hope of maintaining the size of the stock or of assuring the prosperity of the industry by the early 1980s. The pattern of the 1960s and 1970s continued—discovery of a rich bed followed by depletion, followed by discovery of another rich bed, which in turn became depleted. A dense bed of Gulf of Maine scallops, which fishermen discovered in 1979, showed signs of depletion in 1981, and biologists expected any significant fishery to end because the Gulf of Maine had never sustained scallops for long. In the traditional scallop fishing areas of Georges Bank and the mid-Atlantic, the condition of the resource depended on the size of the year classes. Abundant scallop resources made Georges Bank a profitable fishing area for the New Bedford fleet by 1981, but in the mid-Atlantic, catches remained very low.[33]

Landings of sea scallops declined slightly from 1977 through 1980, increased to nearly 9,000 metric tons in 1981, and then declined again to about 7,200 metric tons in 1982. In 1981, revenues were 2 2/3 times the level in 1977, but in 1982, the value of the catch fell to near the 1979 level, about $57 million, almost a 30 percent decline from 1981.[34]

As in the offshore groundfish industry, higher revenues through 1981 did not translate into higher incomes. A crew share in 1981 still could pay extremely well—an average of nearly $35,000 on a group of the highest earning scallop boats—but the crew share fell 6 percent between 1980 and 1981. The same held for returns to capital and management on the highest earning scallop vessels. Their average net return fell about 8 percent between 1980 and 1981.[35]

The reasons incomes began to fall were similar to the reasons ground-fish industry incomes declined. The number of vessels in the scallop fishery had increased greatly in response to high incomes around the time the 200-mile limit went into effect. By 1979, 200 boats were using scallop dredges in New England. Of these, 125 derived most of their gross stock from scallops, and many were offshore vessels. Only 86 scallop dredges had worked in New England in 1976, and only 46 had earned their major gross stock from scallops. Higher costs and the recession helped to squeeze profits and lower fishermen's earnings by the early 1980s.[36]

THE INSHORE FISHERIES

The resource management policies also affected the inshore fishery because the groundfish quotas applied to inshore fishermen as well. The scallop management plan affected inshore fishermen in Maine who were harvesting an unusually rich bed of small scallops in the Gulf of Maine. Also, the groundfish quotas implemented by the council caused many offshore fishermen to move into areas close to shore once the quotas were met beyond three miles from the coast, thereby interfering with the inshore catch.

Price increases improved the incomes of inshore fishermen in the late 1970s. A survey of inshore fishermen in southern New England in 1979 and 1980 showed that full-time fishermen earned more than $23,000 in a year; fishermen who worked part time earned an average of over $16,000.[37]

Summary

The economic trends in the New England fishing industry examined in this chapter highlight a number of significant features. Changes in the condition of the fish stocks meant that catch levels varied greatly. Overfishing by both foreign and American fleets had prolonged effects on catch, and shifting resource management policies contributed to extreme month-to-month fluctuations, but failed to prevent continued overfishing.

At the same time, demand for fish and shellfish grew, so prices generally increased and total revenues rose. As higher prices led to higher incomes for boat owners and fishermen, however, additional vessels and fishermen came into the industry and individuals' incomes deteriorated.

The two major sectors of the industry experienced these changes very differently. In the inshore industry, as the availability of fish varied and as incomes rose and fell, adjustments occurred quickly. Fishermen shifted to harvesting other species, new fishermen entered the industry, or fishermen spent more time at shore jobs or left the industry altogether. Because fixed investments in boats and gear were small, the inshore fleet readily shed or added capital in response to economic change. This flexibility kept incomes more stable in the inshore industry than in the offshore sector.

In the offshore industry, in contrast, the changes meant booms and busts. Despite isolated examples, such as the migration of offshore scalloping vessels and crew to Alaskan fishing grounds, redeployment of vessels and crew in the offshore fishing sector is the exception rather than the rule. During the 1960s, when incomes were very low in groundfishing, few vessels left the industry. When incomes rose in the mid-1970s, fishermen and boats entered the industry, but at a slower pace than in the inshore industry, so that those already in the industry experienced very high earnings for several years. As incomes declined with the entry of new vessels and increases in fishing costs, movement out of the industry was very slow. Indeed, after the boom had ended, new boats continued to enter the industry because of the lag between orders and deliveries of vessels. In scalloping as well, few vessels left the industry in years when severe depletion meant lower incomes for boat owners and fishermen, and in periods of sustained prosperity, new boats and fishermen came into the fishery. As subsequent chapters show, capital and labor in the offshore sector, particularly in finfishing, are firmly attached to the industry during periods of decline, and the downward flexibility of this sector is diminishing.

The offshore industry's response to economic change cannot be studied regionally or through aggregate statistics. What is required is an in-depth examination of the economic behavior of the industry. Accordingly, the following chapter explores the microeconomy of fishing through a study of the industry as it operates in the ports of Gloucester and New Bedford.

THREE

The Structure of the Fishing Industry in Gloucester and New Bedford

Although all New England fishing ports have some elements of production, marketing, and labor relations in common, each port has its own identity as an economic system within the fishing industry. Ports specialize in particular species and their fleets fish in different grounds. There are variations in size of vessel and type of gear among New England's fishing ports. There are also differences among ports in the age, education, and ethnicity of the fishing industry's labor force and in its attachment to the industry. Similarly, the ways of adjusting to economic change, the causes for inflexibility in resources committed to the industry, and the consequences of change for jobs and income in the industry are not uniform throughout the New England region. Understanding economic adjustments in the industry, therefore, requires a familiarity with the circumstances of specific ports.

New England's two largest offshore fishing ports, Gloucester and New Bedford, have been selected for detailed analysis. These two ports together account for more than half of New England's large-boat fleet, more than half of the value of the overall catch, and almost two-thirds of New England's fish-processing activity.[1]

The fishing industries in the two ports differ in their pattern of labor recruitment and staffing, in their labor-management institutions, in the ethnic backgrounds of the fishermen, and in the species of fish harvested. In Gloucester, Italians dominate fishing, whereas in New Bedford, Portuguese, Norwegians, and Yankees are the important ethnic groups. Union organization among fishermen plays a much more important role in New Bedford than it does in Gloucester. New Bedford is the major scallop port of the North Atlantic, and scallops represent about half the value of New Bedford's landed catch. Gloucester's fishing industry produces a negligible amount of scallops and relies almost entirely on several varieties of finfish.

This chapter examines the recent economic experience of the fishing industry in these two ports in order to illustrate the types of structural differences that have emerged between them. This will set the stage for the analysis of adjustments in jobs, income, and the labor force in subsequent chapters.

Gloucester, founded in 1642, is one of New England's oldest and most important ports.[2] Originally, mackerel and cod were the major catch, hand lines the fishing method, and salting the means of processing. Salted fish from Gloucester were sold in both American and European markets.

The industry in Gloucester has faced several periods of substantial change in markets and technology. Early in the nineteenth century, it experienced a sustained decline in fishing, halted only by government subsidy in 1818. Later in the nineteenth century, the introduction of trawls or nets towed behind sail-powered vessels contributed to the expansion of fishing activity, as did the use of ice for preserving fresh fish and the development of rail networks for transport. By the mid-1800s, Gloucester was the largest fishing port in the United States, possessing a fleet of 341 schooners and a large salted fish operation.

Fresh fish are now a major portion of the industry's sales and frozen-fish products have replaced salted products. Haddock and cod are the most important species in the Gloucester catch, with flounder a distant third. Today, Gloucester shares the stage with New Bedford as the leading fishing port in New England.

In the latter part of the eighteenth century, New Bedford developed its famous whaling industry which thrived until the last quarter of the nineteenth century. By the mid-nineteenth century, whaling made New Bedford the fourth most important United States fishing port, with an estimated 324 whaling ships employing 10,000 seamen. As whaling declined, fishing ceased to play a significant role in the local economy in the late nineteenth and early twentieth centuries. During the 1920s the fishing industry revived somewhat, but its catch was sold in New York. In the late 1930s, the industry grew rapidly following development of a local filleting operation and the introduction of refrigerated trucking to the Fulton Fish Market in New York City.

Since the 1920s, the New Bedford fleet has specialized in yellowtail flounder, scallops, haddock, cod, and other flounders. New Bedford is now a major fresh-fish processing center, with distribution networks to all major East Coast cities. Unlike Gloucester, New Bedford lacks a significant frozen-fish processing industry.

Size of the Industry

Gloucester's fishing fleet consists of somewhat more than 200 finfish boats, or "draggers." The New Bedford fleet also has about 200 draggers, but this finfish fleet is augmented by about fifty-five to sixty scallop boats.[3] Almost all these boats fish all year.

In 1980 the landed catch in Gloucester was 95.3 thousand metric tons valued at $34.7 million dollars. New Bedford's weight of catch, 45.4 thousand metric tons, was half that of Gloucester's, but it was valued at $71.3 million dollars, more than twice that of Gloucester.[4] By 1984 New Bedford's landings had passed $100 million dollars in value. The difference in the value of the two catches reflects the importance of high-priced scallops in New Bedford's landings. In 1980, 54 percent of the catch value in New Bedford came from sea scallops, 20 percent from cod and haddock, and the rest from other finfish, primarily yellowtail flounder. In Gloucester, 41 percent of the value came from haddock and cod, 13 percent from flounder, 6 percent from scallops, and the rest from a variety of other fish, such as whiting, redfish, hake, cusk, and squid. The fishing labor force was approximately 1,000–1,100 in New Bedford, and slightly under 1,000 in Gloucester.[5]

The landed fish are processed and distributed by about twenty fresh-fish processors and wholesalers in New Bedford, and ten processors and wholesalers in Gloucester. Over 90 percent of the fresh fish landed in both ports is processed and distributed as fresh whole or filleted fish. In New Bedford almost all the scallops are also packaged and distributed fresh. The fresh fish processing industry employs approximately 1,000 workers in New Bedford and from 200 to 600 workers in Gloucester, depending on the season.

Gloucester also has a significant frozen-fish processing sector with seven frozen-fish processors employing about 2,000 workers. In New Bedford there is only one such processor, employing about 250 people. These processors perform secondary processing—cutting, breading, and repackaging—using frozen blocks of fish imported primarily from Canada, Iceland, Korea, Scandinavia, and Poland. The economic activity of these processors is largely independent of the fishing activity of the New England fleets.

Industry Trends

The second half of the 1970s was a period of relative prosperity in the aggregate for the fishing industries in both ports, but over the last fifty years the industry has been marked by frequent fluctuations. Major declines occurred in Gloucester in the early 1920s, early 1930s, early 1950s, and throughout the 1960s. Total tonnage landed in 1969 was a third that of 1960. As the previous chapter indicated, both Gloucester and New Bedford suffered heavily when foreign fishing fleets competed for catch in the offshore fishing grounds in the 1960s and 1970s. This decline was reinforced in New Bedford by a decline in the scallop fishery.

The financial situation in both ports improved during the 1970s (see table 3–1). This improvement was due to greater catches of fish and scallops, combined with generally rising absolute and relative prices. Catch value approximately quadrupled in New Bedford and Gloucester. Adjusting for inflation, this represents a rise of about 70 percent in the real value of the catch.

Table 3–1 shows how the variation in fishing activity was reflected in the employment and earnings figures for the fishing industry in the two ports. Most of the expansion of crew that occurred in the late 1970s came from younger members entering the industry and through immigration of Portuguese and Italians. Employment grew in processing as well, but less dramatically. Until 1980 total payrolls in fishing rose more rapidly than employment, as average earnings also increased. Average annual earnings in the fishing industry increased by 30 percent in New Bedford between 1976 and 1979 and by 35 percent in Gloucester.

In addition to the long-term and year-to-year fluctuations in the fishing industry, there is considerable seasonal variation. Although the offshore fleet fishes for twelve months, trips are generally shorter and less frequent during the winter, and additional boats may operate in good weather. Moreover, some species of fish are available only in the summer. As a result, much more catch is landed in the summer.[6]

Seasonality in catch translates directly into seasonal shifts in the demand for fresh-fish processing as well. The processing labor force, par-

TABLE 3–1   Catch, Value, Employment, and Earnings in Fishing for the New Bedford and
Gloucester Labor Market, 1970–1980

	Catch (in thousand tons)	Value (in millions)	Average employment	Average earnings (in thousands)
NEW BEDFORD				
1970	50.3	$19.6	1,351	$ 8.2
1971	33.6	16.4	1,263	8.0
1972	27.7	18.3	1,237	9.3
1973	28.6	17.4	1,132	9.7
1974	30.4	21.4	1,165	10.8
1975	30.8	31.3	1,222	13.5
1976	29.0	39.2	1,266	16.4
1977	34.5	43.2	1,230	19.6
1978	32.7	54.6	1,221	22.2
1979	39.0	67.4	1,881	21.2
1980	45.4	71.3	2,039	18.2
GLOUCESTER				
1970	41.7	$ 8.4	655	$ 8.2
1971	50.3	7.9	649	7.2
1972	50.8	9.6	611	8.9
1973	59.0	12.2	585	11.8
1974	54.0	11.4	618	10.4
1975	57.2	14.5	642	12.0
1976	65.3	16.5	692	13.3
1977	68.5	21.5	752	14.7
1978	83.9	28.9	784	17.5
1979	72.7	29.7	855	18.0
1980	95.3	34.7	950	15.4

SOURCE: Research Department, Massachusetts Division of Employment Security; L. J. Smith and S. B. Peterson, "The New England Fishing Industry: A Basis for Management," Technical Report 77–57, Woods Hole, Mass.: Woods Hole Oceanographic Institution, 1977; U.S. Department of Commerce, National Marine Fisheries Service, Fisheries of the United States, Current Fisheries Statistics no. 8100, April 1981, p. 5.

ticularly in Gloucester, is readily expandable during the summer, and processors can also operate multiple shifts or use overtime whenever the volume of catch necessitates it, thereby eliminating the need to invest in new capital facilities.

The Production Process in Fishing and Fish Processing

The fishing fleet of Gloucester consists primarily of large off-shore draggers. These boats average about eighty to ninety feet in length, and displace 60 to 150 gross registered tons. The New Bedford fleet consists of similar vessels and is augmented by the scallop fleet which has boats comparable in size to the offshore draggers. All these boats fish on multiday trips, twelve months of the year. In addition, in both cities there are a few smaller, inshore boats—displacing less than 60 gross registered tons—that primarily make day trips.[7]

FINFISHING

The larger finfish boats in the Gloucester and New Bedford fleets fish in the areas of Georges Bank, Nantucket Shoals, and the Great South Channel most of the year. The outer (northeast) ridge of Georges Bank is the farthest, but among the most fertile, of the fishing areas. This area was lost to United States fishermen in 1984 when the boundary between the United States and Canada in these waters was established by the International Court of Justice. Getting to these areas involves one full day's steaming each way. Fishing trips last from five to thirteen days depending on distance to the fishing ground from port, weather, and abundance of catch.

There are two types of finfish boats: side trawlers and stern trawlers. A side trawler works its nets off the side of the boat and a stern trawler sets its nets from the stern. The stern trawler is the newer of the two and typically has a steel hull, whereas the older trawlers are made from wood. Both types are draggers and the method of catching fish involves the dragging of otter trawls (large conical nets) along the sea bottom to capture ground-feeding species of fish. Midwater fish such as mackerel, herring, and whiting are caught by trawls set at varying depths in the water, or by purse seines.

Crew sizes on the draggers presently range from five to seven men. Some of the more modern, highly mechanized boats can go out with less than four men, but this is uncommon. The crew size has declined from earlier decades, when as many as twelve men worked on draggers, both because the volume of catch declined and because of technical changes. The introduction of the stern trawler, reels for coiling nets, and remote control equipment such as winches has reduced the manning requirements of the boats. As catch has grown in the last several years, crews have not returned to previous levels.

Crew members may shift through several of the tasks on a trip, and one individual is likely to have the skills to work many of the tasks of the boat. The skills of the captain, however, are critical to vessel produc-

New Bedford steel stern trawler rigged to
fish Georges Bank.
Photo: Susan Peterson

tivity. These skills can only be learned by working in the pilot house and the captain controls who learns the skills. Other skills, in particular the special skills of setting and mending nets, are learned gradually by one crew member from another.

SCALLOPING

Scallop boats steam from New Bedford to two major fishing areas, Georges Bank and the Great South Channel, located north of Nantucket Island. In the past, New Bedford scallop boats have fished as far away as the mid-Atlantic waters off New Jersey and Maryland when the scallop catch was low in the Northeast Atlantic region. In the early 1980s, the mid-Atlantic areas have not yielded catches sufficient to warrant such long trips.

The boats used for scalloping are large stern or side trawlers, but different gear are used for harvesting scallops than for groundfish in New England. Because the bottom is sandier in mid-Atlantic states, scallops are caught with regular trawls. The boats harvest scallops by towing a dredge with attached chain bags along the bottom of the fishing areas. The dredge is hauled up and emptied on the deck of the boat, and the scallops are picked over and separated from the debris dredged up with them. The scallop meats are then cut from the shell by the shuckers (or "cutters"). A good shucker will cut about four buckets, eighty pounds each, of scallops in a six-hour shift. The scallop meats are then packed in forty-pound bags and stored in the hold of the boat.

Scallop trips are typically ten days long. Two days are spent in traveling, and eight days are spent fishing. Trips are separated by a five-day layover, so a typical boat makes two trips per month. The eight-day period for fishing and five for layover is presently part of the union contract and has been a customary fishing practice for a long time. This sequence is intended to maintain the quality of the catch by limiting storage time, and also to stabilize the catch by preventing gluts and depletion. In 1981 scallop trips yielded a catch of over eight metric tons per trip, the highest in several decades. By 1985 catches were down to less than two metric tons per trip.

Crew size on the scallop boats ranges from nine to thirteen, and a typical crew is eleven or twelve. Scallop boats can operate with as few as four crew members if scallops are not shucked on board, but a crew of nine or ten appears to be the more common lower bound on large scallop boats.

Wooden offshore side trawler
heading for Georges Bank.
Photo: National Marine Fisheries Service

The skills needed on the scallop boat involve navigation, engine and gear maintenance, setting and hauling gear, cooking, and shucking. A major distinction in tasks between scalloping and groundfishing is in preparation of the catch. The diverse and specialized tasks for handling finfish are not necessary for scallops. Scallops are shucked on board while the boat continues to dredge. Shucking is physically demanding, repetitive work, the main requirements for which are dexterity, stamina, and strength. The majority of the scallop-boat crews are shuckers who do not typically learn the skills required for operating the boat. Few scallop shuckers have experience on draggers, and hence have not acquired the more varied and detailed skills of groundfishing.

FISH PROCESSING

There are two types of fish processing in both New Bedford and Gloucester, processing of fresh fish and processing of imported frozen fish. The fresh-fish processors are closely connected to the operation of the local fishing industry; the frozen-fish processors are not. Fresh-fish processors operate primarily in two product areas: (1) sorting, packing, and shipping of whole fresh fish, usually to Boston or the Fulton Fish Market in New York City; and (2) filleting, packing, and shipping fresh fillets, either to Boston, New York, Philadelphia, and Baltimore, or to retail outlets throughout the country. In addition, there is a small amount of freezing of whole or filleted fresh fish. Processors specialize in round-bodied fish (such as haddock, cod, and pollock) or flatfish (flounders).

Although much of the operation of fresh-fish processing is similar in the two ports, aspects of the organization of the industry differ. The fish dealers in Gloucester include wholesalers, smaller processors employing perhaps fifteen to twenty-five people to cut and pack fish, and larger processors who employ sixty to eighty people.

The scale of the operation is generally larger in New Bedford. Most of the processing is done by the dozen larger processors who employ from 75 to 140 people. One of the larger established processors in New Bedford employs about 135 people, and estimates that with 100 people he will typically process about 100,000 pounds of fish per day. There is also a fringe of very small processors who periodically enter and leave the market.

The sales transactions between the boats and the fish dealers also operate somewhat differently in the two ports. In New Bedford, much of the fleets' catch is sold daily through a formal market, the New Bedford auction, operated by the New Bedford Fishermen's Union and the City of New Bedford. New Bedford processors and wholesalers buy through the auction, from wholesalers, and directly from fishermen.

The larger established New Bedford processors make some use of Canadian fish and, to a lesser extent, fish landed in Maine and Rhode Island. The processors indicate that they are primarily concerned with maintaining steady supplies of fish for their larger customers, and that they therefore are willing to buy and ship Canadian fish trucked to them from the Maritime Provinces if the local catch is low.

Although in the late 1940s and early 1950s, Gloucester had a selling room operated by the Gloucester Chapter of the Atlantic Fishermen's Union, such an arrangement does not operate today.[8] A set of less formal, more individualized arrangements exists in which individual boats usually sell to a single dealer. Some dealers have contracts with particular boats, although most arrangements are based upon verbal understandings rather than on written contracts. Some of the dealers assist boats through special arrangements, such as loans or discounts on supplies to help ensure steady fish supply. Prices are variations on the daily Boston auction price, marked down for transportation costs, as most of the fish are ultimately shipped to the Boston area.

In recent years, Gloucester processors have increased their purchases of fresh Canadian fish in response to lower domestic landings and increasing domestic demand for fresh fish. This is especially the case during the winter months when the local catch is down.

When the boats arrive in port, they are unloaded by "lumpers" or stevedores and the catch is graded or "marked" and sold to one of the fish wholesaler/processors. In New Bedford, there are about 125 to 140 lumpers who unload the boats. Lumping is not full-time work. Lumpers in New Bedford work from the early morning until the boats' catch is unloaded, usually before noon. Individual lumpers are tied to specific boats, so that of the 125 to 140 lumpers in New Bedford, only 30 to 40 will be working at any particular time when their boats are unloading. In Gloucester, there are only about 50 lumpers, because Gloucester fishermen often unload their own boats.

The jobs in nonautomated processing plants are for cutters, who are the highest skilled and paid, trimmers, weighers, packers, skinning machine operators, and some laborers who haul and load boxes. In more automated plants, machines have been introduced to do the skinning, cutting, and filleting tasks. There are separate machines for heading, for filleting, and for skinning, and the machinery is specialized for either groundfish or flatfish. Some of these plants still use hand labor, to avoid waste, for the more expensive fish.

The structure of jobs for fresh-fish processing workers is essentially the same in Gloucester and New Bedford. In Gloucester, for example, the three largest fresh-fish processors each employ a regular work force of around seventy-five, two-thirds of whom are packers, 15 percent, cutters, and the remainder, general laborers who operate forklifts, haul boxes, and the like. Smaller fresh-fish processors each employ as few as fifteen cutters and packers year-round and family businesses may be as small as four. Fish wholesalers average six to twelve laborers and truckers.

Although scallops represent only about 10 percent of the poundage processed in New Bedford, they account for about 50 percent of the gross value, due to the high price per pound. Very little value added occurs in the processing of scallops, because the processing tasks are mainly sorting, washing, and packaging. The mark-up of processed scallops is relatively small. Despite the critical dependence of New Bedford's fishermen on scallops for the bulk of the value of their catch, scallops contribute a relatively small fraction to the total profits of the processing business. Estimates based upon interviews suggest that scallops represent no more than 5 to 10 percent of the profits of those processors who deal extensively in scallops. Interviews suggest that of the roughly 9,000 metric tons of scallops landed in New Bedford in 1981, three-quarters went directly into the fresh-fish market without any processing.

Frozen-fish processing is a much different operation than fresh-fish processing. The frozen-fish processors tend to operate year-round with only some seasonality resulting from higher demand for frozen fish during the winter months. The supply of fish to be processed arrives almost entirely as frozen slabs and blocks. The processors cut the slabs and prepare the fish for frozen meals. The skills involved do not overlap with those of fresh-fish processing. These processors occasionally make local purchases when the local fish prices are low, but they generally are "enclave" businesses whose fate is almost entirely divorced from the experience of the local fishing sector. This is a small part of fish processing in New Bedford, but in Gloucester, frozen-fish processing employs about four times as many people as fresh-fish processing does.

Lumpers offloading yellowtail flounder from a
New Bedford side trawler.
Photo: Susan Peterson

Ownership and Financing of the Fishing Fleet

Most groundfish boats in Gloucester are family owned and operated, typically by first- and second-generation Sicilians. Family relationships influence both the operation and the financing of the boats. In New Bedford, ethnicity and family also play a role in the organization and operation of groundfishing, but much less so in scalloping. The most important ethnic group in terms of numbers in New Bedford groundfishing is first- and second-generation Portuguese. The Portuguese do not completely dominate the finfishing sector in New Bedford as the Italians do in Gloucester, but they represent most of the expansion in boats and employment in groundfishing in the last decade.

A substantial fraction of the New Bedford scallop fleet is owned by established New Bedford fishing families. In addition, some boats are owned by fish dealers or by syndicates of investors. The majority of boats are owned by people who own more than one boat and the largest owner has a fleet of five boats.

The scallop boats are typically operated at sea by a captain hired by the owner, who is then responsible for selecting the crew. Crews tend to be ethnically diverse, although the Portuguese are the most numerous ethnic group. Owners are more or less involved in the decisions about fishing areas, equipment, maintenance, and facilities for crew, depending on their experience in fishing. Some owners hire "shore captains" to handle these decisions. Hence, there is often a distinction between boat ownership and boat crew, and a more formal employment structure replaces the family work structure typical of groundfishing.

The aggregate figures on the number of vessels and fishing trips in each port also suggest considerable flexibility in the addition of capital resources to the industry in response to increases in the volume and value of catch. The most recent example was the expansion and upgrading of both the Gloucester and New Bedford fleets in expectation of continued high prices and increased availability of catch following the imposition of the 200-mile fishing limit. However, because the fishing industry and the fish-processing industry are subject to significant output fluctuations, substantial declines in catch threaten those operations whose debt payments are a large portion of normal revenues. Furthermore, during bad years it is difficult to transfer capital out of the industry.[9]

Family relationships play an important role in boat financing in

Gloucester and New Bedford. Recent immigrant families, either Italian in Gloucester or Portuguese in New Bedford, utilize the family and community ethnic structure to accumulate the savings required for an investment in fishing. By maintaining high rates of savings within a family and by pooling family assets, both self-financing and bank borrowing are facilitated. This family structure of pooled income and assets, as well as the strong cultural commitment to fishing, implies a more resilient ability to endure revenue fluctuations than normal business borrowers, but also implies that capital will be slow to leave the industry following a more permanent downturn.

The expansion of the fleet during the 1976–1980 period illustrates the financial structure of the fishing fleet. Capital was drawn into the industry during this period in a variety of ways, with varying debt burdens. The major source of borrowing was banks. Although specific figures for Gloucester and New Bedford are not readily available, an inventory of all New England vessels indicates that banks financed about 60 percent of the mortgages taken on boats between 1976 and 1980.[10] The Production Credit Association, a federal lending agency, financed another 15 to 17 percent of the mortgages. Two other government sources of funds, the Small Business Administration and Fishing Vessel Obligations Guarantee Loans, financed 7 and 5 percent of the mortgages, respectively.

Local banks, sometimes in conjunction with federally sponsored loans, were able to offer the best terms to the owners of the new large offshore boats. Among the large otter trawl boats in New England, the ratio of finance payments to the gross receipts of the boat averaged about 15 to 18 percent, although some boats, particularly those financed by credit companies, had debt burden ratios as high as 40 percent.

Interviews suggest that two-thirds of the large boats in Gloucester are financed with some loans, and the remainder solely by family funds. Gloucester banks, the major source of local financing, confine their loans to large, family-owned boats with backing from the Small Business Administration or the National Marine Fisheries Service. These agencies guarantee bank loans up to 87.5 percent of the loan value, but regulations, such as those of the Small Business Administration, require that a boat owner show profitable performance for the three previous years, promise of future earnings, and a record of repaying previous bank loans. Only the owners of the largest and most successful vessels in the Gloucester fleet meet these standards.

Most New Bedford boats, whether for scalloping or finfishing, are owned by local families and long-established fishing businesses. In recent years there has been an expansion of the scallop fleet, but interviews with local boat owners and bankers indicate that more than three-quarters of the newly acquired boats are owned by families or enterprises that already have one or two boats. Typically, these owners have been able to save sufficiently to purchase the boats with substantial amounts of their own retained funds. Some of the boats, for instance, were acquired with mortgages amounting to only 20 percent of purchase price. Some of the remaining New Bedford boats, however, have been financed with more borrowed funds, up to 80 percent of the purchase price. Fewer than 20 percent of the New Bedford owners have sought money through government-sponsored loan programs. Most of the loans have been granted by local commercial banks.

Labor Management Structure

There are substantial differences in the way in which labor management relations are conducted in the fishing sector of the two ports. In Gloucester, the fishermen's union once played a major role in the determination of pay and working conditions. [11] With the increasing dominance of Italian family-owned vessels in the Gloucester fleet, trade unions and collective bargaining have been gradually replaced by kinship-based practices. Today, the fishermen's union plays little role in influencing the jobs and income of Gloucester fishermen. The union, to the extent it has a function in the industry, now serves primarily as a social organization.

In contrast, the New Bedford Fishermen's Union has been a more active and aggressive participant in the economic life of the industry. Founded in 1938, the union was originally an offshoot of the Atlantic Fishermen's Union in Boston founded one year earlier. It subsequently became affiliated with the Seafarers International Union, and in 1977 became an affiliate of the International Brotherhood of Teamsters. In 1985 members voted to return to SIU. The union is strongest in scalloping, but finfishing vessels are being recruited actively.

Some New Bedford boat owners are represented by the Seafood Producers Association, although most have no formal representative in port. The Seafood Producers Association was organized in 1938 in response to unionization of fishermen and has always negotiated the collective bargaining agreement with the Fishermen's Union. In addition, it is involved in marketing, promotion, and lobbying on behalf of the fishing industry.

Rates of pay for fishermen are determined by a "lay" system, which links earnings to the value of each trip's catch, and equalizes the share of each trip's revenue among crew members. Because the lay system links pay directly to the value of the catch, fishermen have an immediate stake in the price paid.

Much of the union activity in each of New England's ports has historically centered on promoting competition among dealers to get "fair" prices for landed fish.[12] This was done by establishing union-operated auction rooms in which dealers openly bid for each boat's catch. In Gloucester the formal auction has disappeared along with the economic role of the fishermen's union, but in New Bedford the union-supported auction is still important. The auction system centralizes the sale of a substantial fraction of the catch and places some economic pressure on the nonunion boats.

Onshore work is organized in both ports. In Gloucester, the larger fresh-fish processors and the frozen-fish processors are under union contract. The principal processing unions in Gloucester are the United Food and Commercial Workers International Union and the Amalgamated Meat Cutters and Butcher Workmen of North America.

Lumpers in New Bedford are represented by the International Longshoremen's Association. Their contract is negotiated with the Seafood Producers Association. Because lumping is only part-time work, and in a pinch can be done by boat crews, lumpers are not a crucial part of the labor management landscape. Their rate of pay depends on the amount of fish off loaded, and the job assignment—hold, deck, winch, or chute.

Prior to 1981, three-fourths to five-sixths of the New Bedford processing workers were represented by the Seafood Workers Union, affiliated with the International Longshoremen. In 1981 an unsuccessful strike by processing workers over rates of pay and variability of employment substantially weakened the union, and presently less than one-fifth of the workers are unionized. Hourly rates of pay were reduced by 15 to 30 percent, even for those workers still under a collective bargaining agreement. Union influence in New Bedford is now very weak and processors have greater flexibility in scheduling work and setting pay.

Summary

New Bedford and Gloucester are the two largest fishing ports in New England. The large-boat, offshore fisheries which account for the bulk of New England's fish harvest are concentrated in Gloucester and New Bedford. The industries in both ports expanded in terms of catch, revenues, jobs, and boats during the latter part of the 1970s. During the early 1980s the situation was uneven, but overall the industry was more stable in comparison to the 1970s.

The Gloucester fishing industry specializes in groundfish, and first- and second-generation Sicilians dominate the industry. The system of close family relationships has replaced union organization as the structuring institution in the labor market for fishermen. Boats are primarily owned by the people who captain and crew them, and shared family savings and assets provide the basis for financing them.

The New Bedford fishing industry includes both groundfishing and scalloping, and almost all New England's scallop catch is accounted for by the New Bedford fleet. Fishermen are more ethnically diverse in New Bedford, although the Portuguese have become the most significant group in groundfishing, both owning and crewing the boats. The Portuguese are also represented among scallop crews, but the scallop boats are owned by older New Bedford families and other investors, and are operated mostly by hired captains. The Fishermen's Union plays a less active role in New Bedford than it did in the late 1970s, perhaps because of the growing number of family-dominated boats in New Bedford.

In each port, the catch is processed and distributed by a local fish-processing industry whose activities are closely tied to the local fleet. This processing activity is distinct from the secondary processing of imported frozen fish, which also occurs in both ports.

The differing technology of groundfishing versus scalloping has resulted in differing skill mixes between the two groups of fishermen. These skill differences are important in understanding the adjustments that are made in each fishery as catch fluctuates. However, as will be argued in chapter 5, the employment systems that ultimately determine how adjustments are made reflect not only the technology of the industries, but also the ethnic patterns that have evolved in the fishing communities.

FOUR

Fishermen, Processing Workers, and Their Jobs

Statistics on catch and employment, and descriptions of the structure of the fishing industry in Gloucester and New Bedford provide only limited insights into the characteristics of workers and the nature of the work involved. Fishing is not just a job, it is a way of life. Attachment to fishing as an occupation can be attributed to the economic potential of the industry, strong ethnic and family traditions, and a penchant for a style of work not provided by most onshore jobs.

This chapter addresses a series of work-force issues—labor force characteristics, ethnicity, job attachment and job satisfaction, skill development, and work organization—which contribute to the social structure of the fishing industry.[1] An appreciation of this structure is central to understanding processes of adjustment within local port economies.

The Fishing Industry's Labor Force

The labor force in the fishing industry in the two ports is poorly educated, both in absolute terms and relative to the surrounding community. In the Gloucester Labor Market Area (LMA), in 1980, less than 14 percent of the commercial fishermen had education beyond high school and 43 percent had not graduated from high school.[2] In the New Bedford Standard Metropolitan Statistical Area (SMSA), educational disadvantage was even more dramatic. The median level of education among commercial fishermen was only nine years, three less than in Gloucester. Less than 10 percent had formal education beyond high school and over two-thirds had not graduated from high school (see table 4–1).

Many of the fishermen have only limited experience with other occupations. In Gloucester, approximately one-third of a group of fishermen surveyed in the late 1970s had no experience with jobs other than fishing.

This chapter was written by Susan Peterson and Richard Pollnac.

TABLE 4–1   *Educational Attainment of Commercial Fishermen, 1980*

Years of school completed	Gloucester LMA	New Bedford SMSA
8 or less	24.3%	42.3%
9–11	18.9	26.9
12	43.2	21.2
13+	13.5	9.5
Median	12	9

SOURCE: U.S. Census of Population, 1980. Public Use Sample.

The others had had only one or two jobs outside fishing. Lack of alternative work experience can be attributed not only to the positive benefits of fishing, but also to the fact that the skills learned in commercial fishing are not transferable to other occupations.

Even among the Gloucester fishermen who had some work experience outside fishing, the fishing connection remained strong. Most nonfishing employment was in activities such as fish processing, unloading, and selling. Less than one-third of the work experience outside fishing included factory work or machine skills and much of this experience was accounted for by multiple jobs held by the same individuals. The remainder of the work experience was largely unskilled or manual (see table 4–2). Thus, fishermen generally lack the education and experience to gain any but the most low-skilled entry jobs elsewhere in their communities.

TABLE 4–2   *Distribution of Lifetime Alternative Work Experience of Gloucester Fishermen*

Fish processing, distribution, and supply	24.6%
Factory	18.4
Machine and metal working	9.2
Construction	9.2
Restaurant	7.7
Boat repair	3.1
Casual	4.6
Military	12.3
Miscellaneous	10.8

Number of fishermen = 65
SOURCE: Unpublished survey by Margaret Dewar

These education and skill problems are compounded with the disadvantages of age and lack of fluency in English among recent immigrants. Almost half (44.2 percent) of the commercial fishermen in New Bedford were born outside the United States and the bulk of these immigrants are Portuguese. Two-thirds of these immigrants have arrived in the United States since 1960, and four-fifths had five years or less of formal schooling.[3] Gloucester has a much smaller immigrant work force, only 16 percent of all commercial fishermen, but virtually all of these immigrants are Italians who immigrated to the United States after 1960. In addition, about one-fifth of the labor force in Gloucester's fishing industry, and over 40 percent of the fishing labor force in New Bedford, were over forty-five years of age (see table 4–3).

TABLE 4–3   Age of Fishermen, 1980

	Gloucester LMA	New Bedford SMSA
16–19	8.1%	1.9%
20–24	32.4	5.8
25–44	40.5	46.2
45–64	16.2	46.2
65+	2.7	

SOURCE: U.S. Census of Population, 1980. Public Use Sample.

Despite these factors that are generally considered employment handicaps, fishermen are well paid. Median earnings in 1979 in Gloucester and New Bedford were $11,412 and $16,005 respectively. Because some fishermen work part time, and because there are variations in the value of the catch, data on median earnings conceal a broad range of actual earnings. For example, one-quarter of the Gloucester fishermen, and almost half of the New Bedford fishermen, earned $20,000 or more in 1979 (see table 4–4).

TABLE 4–4   Annual Earnings of Commercial Fishermen, 1979

	Gloucester	New Bedford
Less than $10,000	45.4%	26.7%
$10,000–$14,999	15.9	20.0
$15,000–$19,999	13.6	5.0
$20,000–$29,999	13.6	18.3
$30,000+	11.4	30.0
Median Earnings	$11,412	$16,005

SOURCE: U.S. Census of Population, 1980. Public Use Sample.

Our interviews suggest that earnings in excess of $15,000 to $20,000 per year were typical for full-time offshore fishermen during the late 1970s and early 1980s. These incomes are considerably higher than those available elsewhere in the fishing industry, or in other jobs typically filled by workers with similar levels of education and skill. Men earning less than $10,000 per year are largely seasonal or inshore fishermen, many of whom have low-paying jobs outside fishing, who use fishing income to raise their standard of living. Some of these "seasonal" fishermen are the sons of fishing families who work on family boats during the summer school holiday and who may become full-time fishermen. Thus, there is a two-tiered income structure in commercial fishing. The large-boat, off-shore industry provides relatively high earnings and year-round employment while the small-boat, inshore industry yields substantially lower annual income.

The high earnings in the offshore industry would seem to contradict the standard economic model in which one expects to see additional men enter the industry until earnings are reduced to the average earnings found in comparable onshore occupations. There are at least two plausible explanations for the continued presence of such high incomes. First, some of the offshore vessels in Gloucester and New Bedford are high-liners—those vessels that have the highest productivity and income. Because of the high level of skills of their crew and captains, these vessels are able consistently to outperform the rest of the vessels in the offshore fleet. However, these skills are unique to these fishermen, so there is little competition from new or potential entrants into the industry that threatens to bid down these high earnings.[4]

A second explanation is that entry costs are not as low as the economist's model often assumes. As indicated in the previous chapter, the capital investment and fixed costs of a new vessel are substantial, thus entry is limited. Moreover, financing such an investment would be difficult for new fishermen because banks require that a borrower have a confirmed history of profitable fishing in order for him to qualify for a vessel mortgage.

Processing workers earned about $6.00 per hour in Gloucester and $7.00 in New Bedford throughout the early 1980s. Annual earnings of processing workers in Gloucester, however, are generally higher than in New Bedford (see table 4–5) because there is a substantial amount of full-time, year-round employment provided by frozen-fish processing in

TABLE 4–5 *Annual Earnings of Fish-Processing Employees, 1979*

	Gloucester	New Bedford
Less than $5,000	13.9%	29.6%
$5,000–$9,999	37.4	40.7
$10,000–$14,999	25.0	11.1
$15,000–$19,999	11.1	14.8
$20,000+	12.5	3.7
Median Earnings	$9,255	$7,005

SOURCE: U.S. Census of Population, 1980. Public Use Sample.

Gloucester. Fresh-fish processing is highly variable in both ports. In New Bedford, about one quarter of all fresh-fish processing workers are employed for less than half the year.[5] Although comparable data are not available for Gloucester, interviews show that the incidence of part-year employment is higher than in New Bedford.

Ethnicity

Ethnic background plays a particularly important role in the fishing industry. An understanding of this is central to understanding who gets hired and trained, how family income is accumulated, and how attachments to the industry are formed. New England fishermen come from a variety of ethnic backgrounds. Some are recent emigrants—primarily from Italy and Portugal, but also from Norway, Greece, and Canada; some are the sons or grandsons of emigrants from these countries; and some are best defined as "Yankees"—long-time residents of New England descended from English settlers. Their cultural backgrounds—histories, languages, beliefs, myths, expectations, aspirations, and educations—have contributed to the different industry patterns in each port. These cultural and social factors help to explain the present status of commercial fishing and fish processing in Gloucester and New Bedford.

The fishing ports of Gloucester and New Bedford were settled by emigrants from Western Europe. Some of these were fishermen before leaving their homelands and remained fishermen in the United States. Others became fishermen because they found no other comparable employment opportunities. The ethnic history and composition of the fishing industry differ considerably between Gloucester and New Bedford.

TABLE 4-6 Ethnic Background of Commercial Fishermen, 1980

	Gloucester	New Bedford
Italian	45.9%	*
Portuguese	*	36.5%
English	13.5	17.3
French	8.1	11.5
Norwegian	13.5	*
Irish	*	9.6
Polish	*	5.8
All Other	19.0	19.3

*Less than 5%
SOURCE: U.S. Census of Population, 1980. Public Use Sample.

In the eighteenth and early nineteenth centuries, the Gloucester fleet was primarily English. Despite the prosperity of the industry during the nineteenth century, Gloucester fishermen began to counsel their sons to take up other occupations.[6] Disenchantment, combined with a growing fleet, allowed opportunities for new entrants. The earliest immigrants to take advantage of these openings were Scottish and Irish. These were followed during the 1830s by emigrants from the Canadian Maritimes, many of French descent. During the 1850s, Portuguese immigrants began to augment the fleet. By the 1890s, Italian immigrants began to replace the Portuguese, and before the end of the first half of the twentieth century, a large proportion of the fleet was Italian, primarily Sicilian. Only a few fishermen of Portuguese descent remained in the Gloucester fleet.

Today, Italians are the largest ethnic group within the Gloucester fleet, holding almost half of all fishing jobs (see table 4-6). More than 85 percent of the captains are Italian. Of the Italian fishermen, about one-third were born in Italy. The fishermen make distinctions among themselves based on their ties to Italy. One group of fishermen of Italian descent labels itself as "American," yet maintains that it is a part of the "Italian fleet." These fishermen contrast themselves with other fishermen of Italian descent who more recently immigrated to this country. The Italian fleet is predominately Sicilian, although there are a few fishermen and families who have roots in other parts of Italy.

Like Gloucester, New Bedford's ethnic composition has changed over the years. In the colonial period, it was a Quaker-Yankee settlement and this group continued its predominance until well into the nineteenth century. However, the growing whaling industry was in constant need of men and drew upon emigrants from Portugal, Norway, and England, nationalities reflected in the current fishing industry labor force. Information on the distribution of foreign-born New Bedford residents since 1920 shows that the British and Portuguese have been the most numerous immigrants. For more than a century, however, the community has not been a Yankee town.

At present, the dominant ethnic group in New Bedford is Portuguese (see table 4–6) from mainland Portugal and the Azores. There are also substantial numbers of Irish, Polish, and Yankees. Norwegians are substantially represented among captains (approximately 20 percent). About half of the immigrants have been in the United States ten years or less.

The Portuguese fishermen have a closely knit community, partly because many immigrants are not fluent in English. Unlike the first generation of fishermen, who worked as crew on vessels owned by others, some of the second generation own their own boats and have carved out rather specialized niches or fishing strategies in the New Bedford fishing industry. Some of these men have specialized in scallops, some in "mixed fishing"—groundfish in the winter and swordfish in the summer—and others in trash fish. Fifteen years ago very few of the New Bedford fishing boats were owned or operated by fishermen of Portuguese ancestry, but during the 1980s that changed, and now more than half the fleet is owned by ethnic Portuguese.

About 40 percent of the New Bedford captains are Norwegian or Yankee. Norwegian captains have a reputation of being more businesslike and hard-driving than other captains. Their boats fish more days during the year than those of other ethnic groups. At the same time, they have been aggressive about obtaining formal educations for their children, which is reflected in the fact that most of the college-educated fishermen are from Norwegian families and that each year fewer of their children become fishermen.

The Portuguese captains are likely to have crews dominated by their own ethnic group, whereas the Yankee captains have a mix from available ethnic groups. This may be because of language differences; on Portuguese-skippered vessels, the language used is a patois of English and Portuguese even though most crews speak some English. In scalloping, crews are more mixed because the boats are skippered predominantly by Yankees.

Recent Immigrants

Both Italian and Portuguese boat owners sponsor kinsmen in the immigration procedure by guaranteeing them jobs on their vessels. When these immigrants, or their sons, obtain sufficient capital to buy a boat, they continue the tradition by sponsoring more relatives who wish to immigrate. This practice has resulted in entire extended families being dependent on the fishery.

In Gloucester, recent Italian immigrants often fish differently from more established fishermen. Their boats are said to "fish in packs" and until the late 1970s, they concentrated on abundant species with low market value, such as whiting. Now they fish for cod, haddock, mixed groundfish, and some scallops, and compete directly with fishermen from the other New England ports. Despite the fact that recent immigrants have less experience with the fishing grounds, they land substantial amounts of fish because they are willing to fish the hard-bottom areas where more experienced fishermen are less likely to fish.

In contrast, many of Gloucester's established Italian boats have fished the same grounds for years and have detailed knowledge of bottom features and fish locations. They are less likely to get hung-up on either rocks or wrecks and they have fewer "broken" trips than recent immigrants, who lack extensive knowledge of the grounds, tear more nets, and, therefore, make less money.

From the earlier immigrant's perspective the recent immigrants "come over here from the Old Country and can't read or write. They ain't got nothing. They just eat bread and spaghetti. They don't go out. Next thing you know they got their own boat, two houses, and a fancy car." The success of recent Italian immigrants is not appreciated by Italians who have "been here longer." They say that the newcomers are just lucky that fish prices have been high in recent years. Some fishermen of Italian descent avoid the St. Peter's Club (a fishermen's club) since "the recent immigrants have taken over." Some recent Italian immigrants flaunt their wealth, "saying 'Come look at my car' and 'I'm gonna go to Italy.' "[7]

An important variable for the transformation from the category of recent immigrant to "Italian American" is the ability to speak English. All recent immigrants speak Italian or a regional dialect as their first language. "Italian Americans," by contrast, speak English, and their children may not be able to converse freely in Italian.

In terms of understanding employment practices in the fishing industry in Gloucester and New Bedford, ethnicity and immigration play important roles. Immigration is a source of new labor for the fishing industry when it is expanding, but because of kinship ties the immigration process is less likely to be reversed when the industry contracts. Immigration also involves economic guarantees by relatives which often mean legal as well as kinship commitments to provide jobs for immigrants, especially those who have recently arrived. Finally, recent immigrants face special language handicaps, which further confine them to fishing and family networks.

The importance of kinship is most clearly observed in Gloucester because of the dominance of Italian boat owners and crews. Recent immigrants, however, make up a relatively small proportion of commercial fishermen in Gloucester. In contrast, New Bedford has far fewer family boats, but new immigrants constitute a much larger fraction of the fishing labor force. As a result, many immigrants in the New Bedford fishing industry work on vessels owned and operated by persons of different ethnic backgrounds.

Importance of Family and Kinship Ties

Kinship plays an important role in the New England fishery. In New Bedford, 69 percent of the fishermen, both captains and crew, interviewed in 1978 had fathers who fished for a living.[8] Fifty-seven percent of the fishermen had at least one kinsman among the crew they fished with, and 71 percent had been introduced to fishing through a relative. A sample of New Bedford captains in 1981 revealed that 60 percent of their fathers and 34 percent of their grandfathers had fished for a living. Twenty percent of them have sons fishing, 34 percent have brothers now fishing, and nearly 25 percent of them have father or uncles currently working as commercial fishermen.

Like New Bedford, family participation in the Gloucester fishing industry is commonplace. Sons and nephews are expected to work on the boats, wives help with the accounting, and uncles, fathers, and grandfathers provide funding for new boats, as well as advice and representation at shoreside meetings. Kinship also plays an important role in assuring entry into the occupation—71 percent of the captains' fathers fished, as did 47 percent of their grandfathers. Thirty-five percent now have sons in fishing, 24 percent have brothers, 18 percent have uncles, 18 percent have cousins, and 12 percent have fathers working on other Gloucester fishing boats. Although 30 percent of the Gloucester captains are only in their twenties and thirties, they own fishing boats or shares in the boats as a result of the support they receive from their families.

Patterns of Job Finding

Many fishermen tell the story of being initially attracted to the fishing occupation by the enticement of high wages.[9] As one fisherman recalled: "I knew I wasn't gonna make that anywhere else." Fishing is also a highly lucrative summer job; the half-share paid these young men is often worth three or four hundred dollars a week, considerably more than they might expect to earn from a conventional job ashore. During the summer months, crew size on many Gloucester vessels increases by one or two men to accommodate members of the family returning from school. Summer jobs serve the dual purpose of providing a young man with a considerable income and of helping the family. Other fishermen report that they never really decided or intended to fish, but that they "fell into it, or fell back on it."

Sites (the term for jobs on fishing boats) are found mainly through family connections. Fishermen may exploit different parts of their kinship network depending upon what kind of job they are looking for; one year a man may use his mother's family connections to find a job, another year, his wife's family may provide him with more options. Family ties also act as constraints on mobility—some men are tied to boats because of kinship obligations despite the fact that more money or a better life could be had elsewhere. As one man pointed out: "That boat doesn't make any money; it's the captain. If his brother had it, it would make twenty to twenty-five thousand a year (per share), instead of ten. The captain always finds a reason not to fish. And he likes to dress big and act as though he's got lots of money. . . ."[10]

Fishermen and boats acquire reputations. Although family and kinship ties are often critical to getting into the industry, talented fishermen are a scarce resource and a fisherman with a good reputation has no trouble finding a site even without kinship connections. Although kinship ties to a boat, or group of boats, remain strong, fishermen occasionally leave boats because they are dissatisfied with the way the captain runs the boat, because they want to make more money, work with friends, or improve their chances for getting ahead. Sometimes job changing occurs because the personality or morality of the skipper is unacceptable. There are boats in Gloucester that are notorious for taking advantage of crew. Like workers everywhere, fishermen prefer to work in an atmosphere of trust.

Another advantage of having a position or site on a good boat is that the work is easier. The highliners tend to have newer equipment and more back-up gear in case something malfunctions. One fisherman proposed the analogy of efficient boat and crew to a well-balanced baseball team. Another said: "You notice that you're always working harder on a bad boat. The good boat's got depth; all the men know how to work twine."

As in Gloucester, New Bedford fishermen find jobs by exploiting their kin and friendship networks. In many cases, the social contact is both a formal kinship link and an informal friendship link. New Bedford fishermen have also used the Fishermen's Union to help them find jobs. The union hall maintains a list of men looking for sites. In order to remain on the list, a man is expected to check in at the hall a few times a week to say that he is still available.

Captains who need crew also have methods for finding them. The most common way to find a new deckhand is to "put the word out." Skippers of highliners never advertise in the paper and rarely use the union hall. Instead, they depend on being able to hire skilled men seeking jobs once it is known within the port that a site is open. Usually the boat's crew talk about the job among friends and family members, looking for someone with whom they would like to work. The trend in New Bedford is for boats with poor earning power to have more transient crews—and for the captains of these boats to use the union list to find deckhands.

Job Satisfaction

The fishermen differ in their training and experience and in their ability to enter or leave fishing. Crew members, at least theoretically, can more easily seek nonfishing employment than can boat owners and captains who have financial and emotional investments in the industry and who have developed specialized skills that discourage leaving the business. However, recent research shows that most crew are as bound to the industry as are the captains and boat owners.[11]

When a fisherman is at sea, he is more isolated from his family and community than individuals in most other occupations. In spite of the often articulated feelings of isolation, fishermen boast of the independence and freedom not available from other occupations. Yet there is also dependence upon communities, families, and fellow crew. Perhaps this is what enhances the special feeling of closeness among crew members, as well as the willingness to work in concert and to support one another in time of need.

Fishermen on offshore boats—those that fish on six- to ten-day trips on Georges Bank or other offshore grounds—have mixed feelings about the advantages of their work. They are quick to point out that, although they know they are making more money than inshore fishermen, they are away from home for 180 to 220 days of the year. Despite these absences, most fishermen have a preference for the regular pattern of offshore fishing—so many days at sea followed by so many days at home. Except for interruptions due to weather or vessel maintenance, offshore fishing has a regular rhythm known to the crews, the captains, and their families.

Many social scientists have argued that aspects of the occupation of fishing select for a specific type of individual.[12] M. Orbach suggests that the family orientation and personality configuration of fishermen tend "to produce a very strong 'psychological contract' between the individual and his occupation."[13] J. Poggie and C. Gersuny present data that indicate that fishermen "look upon their occupation and gain satisfaction from it in a much different way than do comparable landbound workers."[14] Interviews in Point Judith and New Bedford suggest that fishermen who tried other occupations and returned to fishing did so because of the relative independence and personal satisfaction provided by it.[15] When requested to compare alternative occupations with fishing, a sample of fishermen from New Bedford and Point Judith rated their present style of fishing higher in terms of income, future, personal enjoyment, and independence.

When asked why they became fishermen, a group of captains ranked "independence" as most important (58 percent of the respondents), followed by "fulfilled ambition" (43 percent), income supplement (24 percent), and "peace and quiet" (22 percent). In another study, fishermen

Fisherman with assorted flat fish.
Photo: Richard Allen

were asked what they liked about the occupation of fishing. They listed independence, income, family and social life, and personal enjoyment in that order.[16]

Asked why they fish, fishermen (particularly the crew members) responded that "the money is good." In both Gloucester and New Bedford, a majority of the fishermen surveyed indicated that economic reasons were an important inducement to stay in the industry. "Good income" is the only satisfaction whose importance equals that of "independence" for any group.

When asked to compare fishing with an alternative occupation for which they were qualified, 70 percent of the fishermen rated their alternatives unfavorably: "The only thing I want to do is fish; It's not as good; Not as much money; I'd hate it; I tried factory work once—didn't think much of it; It would be more boring; It wouldn't be as much fun; I'd be lowering myself; They don't have much respect; I hate a roof over my head; There'd be more mental pressure."[17]

Further evidence on the satisfactions of fishing comes from fishermen's wives. In Gloucester and New Bedford about 80 percent of the fishermen are married. A survey of fishermen's wives in a nearby New England port found that two-thirds like the positive effects fishing has on their husbands. They made comments such as: "He's his own boss; he's happy."[18]

Job satisfaction may also be reinforced by the quality of home life when fishermen are ashore. Fishermen's wives not only were positive about the effect fishing had on their husbands, they also reported positive benefits for themselves. One-fifth of the wives felt the occupation afforded them benefits they might not receive from other occupations. Some noted that they liked living near the shore, and others enjoyed the "spontaneity of the unpredictable schedule."[19] Wives also noted that they enjoyed their personal independence and the time they had to themselves when their husbands were at sea. This is important to note because although it is often said that the enforced separation causes complications, the reverse seems to be true.

Women from fishing families who marry fishermen are accustomed to this separation and find support from close kinsmen who are also from fishing families. This adaptation is so effective that some wives note that it is good to have the husband home for a short time, but also good to get him out of the way when he goes back to sea. These attitudes are probably general in fishing communities and have been documented elsewhere.[20]

Fishermen's wives not only adapt to the uncertainties of fishing, they also feel that some aspects of the occupation of fishing improve their relationships with their husbands. Wives are counted upon as sources of information—synthesizers of shoreside information important to the captain or crew, and in some cases, as coworkers doing marketing, bookkeeping, and taxes. This aspect of the occupation enhances the women's feelings that fishing is a partnership. When asked about fishermen's short time ashore, several wives noted: "Couples get along better. There's no time to argue, you have to fit a week's worth of living into two days." "Petty irritations don't have time to grow into full-scale arguments."[21]

The more significant work is for an individual, the more the job functions to integrate him into society. Consequently, individuals such as fishermen whose jobs affect diverse aspects of their lives may be more committed to their occupations than those who regard their work simply as a means of earning a living. When meanings of work become so extensive that there is an erosion of boundaries between work and nonwork activities, an occupation may be properly termed "a way of life."

Skills and Training

Although the vessel provides the basic tool of this trade, the capabilities of the men can differ so much that three to four times the volume of fish landed by one skipper can be landed by another using a similar boat and gear. Part of this difference can be explained by differences in aspirations, expectations, and life-style. Some men fish hard during their early years to ensure a comfortable old age, whereas others fish simply to keep bread on the table. There is also limited evidence that aspirations are linked to ethnicity. For example, L. J. Smith and Susan Peterson found that boats skippered by Norwegian captains in New Bedford had significantly higher incomes than did boats run by captains of any other ethnic group.[22] Skill, however, is the key to success in fishing.

There are sharp distinctions in job duties and skills on a boat. The first job an apprentice fisherman gets is likely to be as deckhand. In this position, he is directed and supervised by more senior members of the crew, but many of the directions are given without much detailed guidance. As he learns the fishing routine, the novice fisherman has several options regarding specialization. These options involve learning the skills of twineman, engineer, cook, and, sometimes, captain. Each of these skills has its own advantage and minor benefits. For example, a cook on an off-shore scallop vessel may not be required to share watch time with other members of the gang, but he is required to meet the crew's needs for sustenance around the clock.

Although deckhands can learn a great deal about the operations of a vessel and its machinery from crew members, the only way to learn about fishing strategies is to communicate with the captain. The captain spends most of his time in the pilothouse. Often he alone monitors the electronic devices used to scan the sea bottom for fish. On some vessels, crew members are permitted in the pilothouse when they are not needed elsewhere. Fishermen who take advantage of opportunities to learn from the captain find out about bottom contours, locations of wrecks, the algorithms of particular tows, the movements of fish, and so forth. It takes a special effort for a fisherman to acquire the knowledge he needs to operate his own vessel successfully.

Kinship also influences training of younger fishermen. Most captains are willing to convey information on strategies and techniques to crew members wanting to improve their chances to become captains. This has been particularly important in the transmission of skills from fathers to sons. Ironically, kinship ties can either inhibit or encourage this process. One fisherman on a boat owned jointly by his father and paternal uncle told how his cousin, who skippered the vessel, kept him from the pilothouse: "He won't let me in the pilothouse. He thinks that if I learn then one day I'll say 'You fish fifty percent of the time and I'll take it out the rest of the time.' Everything I've learned I've had to learn on other boats. You know what I mean?"[23]

Processing

Fish landed at New England fish piers in the early years of this century were either salted in barrels or crated to be shipped throughout the port cities as fresh fish. Salt processing was unskilled and was supplied by a casual work force or by fishermen too old to go to sea. The cutting, packing, chilling and/or freezing of fresh fish was done by the consumer. As the consumers began to demand a more finished fresh or frozen product, processing became a more important part of the fishing industry and the old fishermen were replaced by a more skilled labor force.[24]

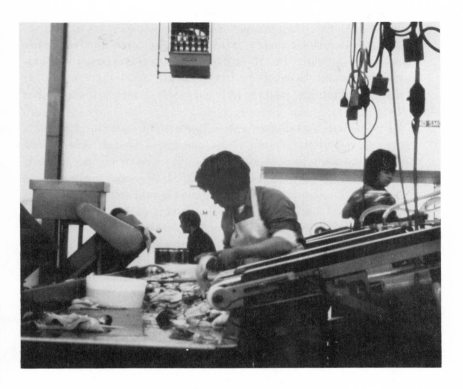

Processing fish fillets in New Bedford.
Photo: Susan Peterson

Women entered the occupation in the 1940s, cleaning fillets, sorting, weighing, and packing. In frozen processing, women worked on breading and cooking fish. In the last fifteen or twenty years, increasing numbers of women have become fresh-fish cutters, the highest paid job on the production line, and the only job in which men still outnumber women.

When fish are landed, the fresh-fish processing plants are busy with unloading, washing, skinning, and filleting activities. Hand- and machine-processing lines operate side by side in many plants. The men work at the chute where the fish come off the boat, doing sorting, icing, and crating jobs and delivering fish to trucks, cold-storage rooms, and processing lines. For processing-plant workers in New Bedford with twenty to twenty-five years of experience, jobs have been stable. Their seniority has guaranteed them work for two-thirds to three-quarters of the year, and they must rely on savings or unemployment benefits only during the slow winter season. Less senior workers have had less predictable incomes from fish-processing jobs, but when there is work it tends to be allocated by seniority among a relatively stable labor force.

In Gloucester, fresh-fish processing is somewhat more informal and there is a greater reliance upon part-time and part-year workers. Because of the extremely seasonal nature of Gloucester processing, employers do not maintain a large, fixed labor force. In the largest plants, as many as 150 additional workers can be called in to process peak volumes. Most of these seasonal workers are women and youths. These employees are considered part time and are not union members. They are paid hourly and can work seven days a week for up to twelve hours a day when catch is abundant. Such production peaks can continue for several weeks. Although the work in processing plants is tedious and repetitive, the atmosphere is lively, particularly during busy periods, and many of the seasonal workers interviewed expressed a strong preference for the seasonal, part-time pattern of work.

Summary

Although work in fish processing is not unlike that in other types of food processing industries involving predominately low-skilled, manual labor, fishing is a different type of business. Work is arduous and requires skill, knowledge, and experience for crew and captain alike.

Fishing requires separation from family and friends on shore, and it can be an isolated and hazardous way of life. It does, however, provide good earning opportunities and a high level of job satisfaction, particularly for a group of workers who may lack formal education and facility with the English language.

Ethnic and kinship ties are an important feature of the fishing industry. The Portuguese are coming increasingly to dominate the New Bedford industry while Gloucester is now almost completely staffed by fishermen of Italian descent. These kinship/ethnic ties are important avenues for the entry of new fishermen into the industry, for the training of fishermen, and for maintaining the economic security of family units.

The combination of high earning opportunities and kinship ties bonds fishermen to their industry. In addition, fishermen appear to find the work itself and the lifestyle of fishing attractive and satisfying. For these reasons, attachment to the industry is very strong and there is considerable evidence that fishermen would be highly resistant to transferring to alternative employment, even at comparable levels of income.

PART TWO

Adjustment to Economic Change

FIVE

Labor Market Structure and Labor Force Adjustment

Neither the structure of the fishing industry nor the characteristics of its labor force reveal how economic change will affect jobs and income in the industry. Because economic change is rarely spread evenly throughout any industry, any change has consequences for the distribution of economic benefits as well as for the level of economic activity. This chapter examines patterns of adjustment to change within the fishing industry. The focus is upon the institutional structure of labor arrangements in fishing and fish processing; on how these arrangements differ by sector and port; and on how they shape employment and earnings in fishing in response to changing economic conditions.

Institutional rules governing employment, pay, and labor market adjustment determine the type and extent of income and employment variation resulting from any given economic change within the industry. Because individuals work under very different types of institutional arrangements, the impact of change is uneven within the fishing industry. As a result, there is not one common pattern of adjustment to change, but several distinct patterns. Knowledge of the principal types of employment systems present in the fishing industry is essential for analyzing the consequences of change within the industry and for predicting the future incidence of change.

Aggregate Labor Force Adjustments

From the data on the fishing industry in New England and in specific ports presented in chapters 2 and 3, it is obvious that employment and the number of fishing vessels expand and contract with the prosperity of the industry. Although such aggregate data might be indicative of considerable flexibility in adjustment to economic change, a closer look at the structure of the labor markets in Gloucester and New Bedford suggests that flexibility is not a universal characteristic of the industry.

The aggregate data, for example, reveal a definite pattern in resource flexibility. In general, the greatest flexibility occurs in the small-vessel (under five tons), inshore sector. The number of fishermen in the small-vessel sector fluctuates more widely than in the large-vessel fleet, and part-time fishermen, who are most closely associated with the small-vessel sector, show the greatest variability in employment in the industry. Moreover, during the growth period of the industry in the late 1970s, the small-vessel sector showed the most rapid response to prosperity, whereas the large-vessel, offshore sector responded with a considerable lag.[1]

This concentration of resource flexibility in inshore fishing is consistent with other types of flexibility. The inshore vessels tend to switch species and gear more readily than offshore vessels in response to changes in price and availability of catch. Moreover, the inshore fleet tends to be more footloose among ports as many inshore fishermen follow the fish on a seasonal basis.[2]

This flexibility is mirrored in the characteristics of the inshore fishermen. In comparison to the offshore fishermen in Gloucester and New Bedford, inshore fishermen are younger, better educated, and more attached to shoreside life, and they have greater work experience outside the industry.[3] Although many inshore fishermen rely exclusively upon fishing as a source of jobs and income, the sector also contains substantial numbers of pleasure boaters who fish as a hobby and occasionally sell their catch.

The inshore, small-vessel sector approximates the economist's model of a competitive, resource-flexible industry, but the situation is markedly different in the offshore sector, which accounts for most of New England's commercial catch. Greater capital requirements make entry and exit more sluggish and inhibit rapid switching among gear and species. Attachment to port and industry is also particularly strong among offshore fishermen, which makes geographic mobility less likely. This stickiness in resource adjustment is further reinforced by the institutional arrangements that determine how income and employment on offshore vessels are affected by economic change.

Although pay, employment, and labor adjustment processes in the fishing industry are influenced by the supply and demand for fish, they are also the result of "institutional" rules. In particular, the rigidity of the labor adjustment process in the offshore sector reflects the institutional arrangements governing employment and pay on particular vessels. These arrangements define who gets hired, how much they are paid, who gets trained, and how economic change is managed at the workplace. These rules and strategies are sometimes codified in collective bargaining agreements, but often they are informal understandings embodied in the custom and traditional practices of each workplace. Whether they are contained in formal contracts or informal understandings, these institutional rules persist unaltered for long periods of time, despite substantial changes in the economic environment.

As will be shown, these rules vary among ports and among vessels within ports, but the variation is systematically related to factors such as unionization, the sector of the industry, the type of boat ownership, the ethnicity of the crew, and the type of fishing conducted. Because of these differences, the incidence of economic change on employment and income must be determined on a port-by-port basis.

Employment Systems in Fishing

The most significant factor differentiating employment systems on fishing vessels is the ethnic character of the boat owners and the work force. As indicated in chapter 4, there are markedly different ethnic patterns of boat ownership and crew membership between Gloucester and New Bedford. Fishing in Gloucester is almost entirely dominated by first- and second-generation Italian families.[4] These families own and captain their own boats and the crews are staffed principally with relatives and friends.

New Bedford is more diverse. Scallop vessels are owned mainly by Norwegians and Yankees (although Portuguese ownership is growing) and crew on these boats are ethnically varied. Many vessels are absentee owned and captains are often unrelated to the boat owners. Some finfishing boats also follow this pattern, but a number of the larger vessels in the finfishing fleet more closely resemble those in Gloucester. This is particularly true for those vessels owned and captained by Portuguese families and manned by their relatives and friends. Ethnic family ownership and operation, by Italians in Gloucester and Portuguese in New Bedford, have become increasingly important in these ports over the past two decades.

"CAPITALIST" SYSTEMS

Those boats in the industry that are staffed largely without regard to ethnicity—principally the smaller boats in the Gloucester fleet owned by non-Italians, the New Bedford vessels owned or operated by Yankees and Norwegians, and the transient vessels from outside New England—are staffed according to "capitalist" employment practices. Under the capitalist system, crew size is adjusted to changes in the availability of catch, vessels are taken in and out of service depending on their overall profitability, and the employment relationship is relatively impersonal.

Although there is considerable continuity in the core crews of capitalist vessels, particularly on the successful highliners, the formal employment relationship is contracted for on a trip-by-trip basis. The decision by individual crew members to remain with a vessel, the willingness of captains to continue to employ specific crew members, and the owners' decisions to continue their vessels in operation are made on the basis of economic considerations, independent of family or kinship connections. Efficiency, merit, and formal seniority govern crew size and staffing decisions. In these respects, capitalist vessels exhibit the same type of flexibility in resource utilization that characterizes smaller, inshore vessels.

KINSHIP SYSTEMS

In contrast to capitalist vessels, the combination of strong kinship ties and the importance of fishing employment for recent immigrants gives a special structure to the labor market for fishermen employed on Italian vessels in Gloucester and on Portuguese vessels in New Bedford. The family-owned Portuguese and Italian fleets follow vastly different employment rules in staffing their boats than do boats in the capitalist sector. In Gloucester, for example, non-Italians rarely find work on Italian vessels unless they possess specialized skills, such as piloting, engine repair, or cooking, or unless the labor market is extremely tight. When the catch is up and employment levels are high, Italian captains often complain about the "shortage" of crewmen. However, this complaint means that they could not find enough men whose families and friends they knew, not that there was a true shortage of experienced job candidates. When asked during interviews which crewmen would be laid off first if catch were to fall, Italian fishermen representing a wide range of boat sizes immediately responded that if layoffs were to occur, they would be limited to non-Italians or other unrelated individuals.

Although experience and ability are not wholly irrelevant on kinship boats, because the presence of an inexperienced crewman can reduce the income of the boat, the preference for kinship in employment is strong. Within wide limits, kinship determines employment priorities, and often the number of crew employed, in Gloucester's Italian fleet. Similar practices can be found on those vessels in the New Bedford fleet that are owned and operated by Portuguese.

Sometimes *recent* immigrants are accorded inferior employment rights on boats owned by better-established fishing families. Nevertheless, they have priority access to jobs and claims to job security in the kinship sector that are unavailable to non-Italians. The Portuguese fleet in New Bedford also tends to follow kinship employment procedures, even though some of these boats are unionized and some staffing practices are also governed by collective bargaining agreements.

Kinship employment systems not only grant family members priority access to job opportunities, they also involve a commitment to provide work for relatives, even in times of substantial declines in catch. This commitment is met by maintaining the size of crews at whatever level is necessary to keep family members employed, regardless of catch, or by rotating family members so that available work and income is shared among all. Kinship vessels deliberately avoid exercising the type of flexibility in staffing that characterizes capitalist vessels.

The Lay System of Pay

On both capitalist and kinship vessels, compensation is governed by a set of arrangements known as the "lay" system—a system that jointly determines the earnings of capital and labor. The lay system is a pay formula that ensures that the operating expenses of the vessel will be met from the proceeds of the catch and that apportions shares of the remaining catch revenue among the captain, crew, and boat owner.

Under the lay system, the income of a crew member depends primarily on the volume and selling price of the catch, on the operating costs of the vessel, and on the number of crew among whom the boat's income must be shared. It contains elements of a piece-rate system in that income is tied, in part, to the volume of catch so that there are incentives for effort and rewards for productivity. Because the lay system involves income sharing, there is an obvious tradeoff between the size of the crew and the income of individual crew members.

The lay system also ensures that both owners and crew share the uncertainty of changes in the volume and selling price of catch. In an industry with high variability in catch and price, the lay system spreads out the economic consequences of variability among the different claimants on boat income.

A final characteristic of the lay system is that certain operating costs are deducted from the value of the catch before disbursements are made to the crew. To some extent this dimension of the lay system insulates vessels from economic shocks and, therefore, helps to stabilize employment.

DIFFERENCES IN LAY SYSTEMS

The specifics of the lay system vary from port to port, between scallop and groundfishing vessels, and even among similar vessels in a single port.[5] Nevertheless, the underlying compensation principles are similar. Deductions are made from the value of the catch to cover fixed and variable costs of operating the vessel and the remainder of the catch revenue is divided, by formula, among the crew.

Lays may be either "clear" or "broken," or a combination of the two. Under a clear lay, the catch revenue is first divided into two parts—one for the vessel and the other for the crew. Specified operating expenses such as fuel, ice, food, and repairs are then deducted in various ways from the vessel and crew shares. The remainder of the vessel's revenue covers depreciation and profits, while the remaining crew portion is divided into shares for the crew members. Under broken lays, operating expenses are first deducted as a block from total revenue and the remainder is apportioned by formula among the vessel and crew. Although relatively simple percentages are used under both lays to divide boat revenue, such as "60–40" or "58–42," the percentage distribution of the total catch revenue is more complicated because of the different ways in which fixed and variable costs are deducted.[6]

The Economic Consequences of Institutional Pay and Employment Practices

In contrast to more familiar wage, piece-rate, or incentive payment arrangements, the lay system might appear to be anachronistic. This view is reinforced by the long tradition of the lay system in the United States, going back to the eighteenth century, and by the presence of similar arrangements on family fishing boats in many developing countries.[7] Nevertheless, the practice seems firmly rooted in capitalist as well as kinship situations and in unionized as well as nonunion vessels. It was in use during the 1920s when the industry was dominated by non-union vessels, many of which were corporate owned, and was preserved when Gloucester and New Bedford became unionized in the 1930s.[8] It continues to be used under the kinship arrangements that have spread into both ports.

Economists who have studied the lay system typically emphasize its role as a mechanism for spreading the risk associated with uncertain revenues among boat owners, captains, and crews.[9] There are, however, other features of the system that have important economic consequences. Because the incomes of both labor and capital are tied to the volume of catch, the lay system provides incentives for effort and rewards productivity and teamwork. It is tempting, therefore, to characterize this system as an efficient, albeit idiosyncratic, compensation arrangement that facilitates crew staffing and productivity, and smoothes the impact of uncertainty.

Recently, however, there are indications that the lay system is not simply an efficient employment contract, but that it may also illustrate how institutional arrangements can persist after their efficiency has diminished. Historically, the lay system caused fishermen's earnings over the long term to fluctuate moderately around those of similarly skilled onshore occupations.[10] This yielded reasonably efficient labor supply incentives. During periods in the 1970s, and more systematically in the 1980s, however, unusually large price increases drove the value of catch up sharply and the lay system's compensation formulas automatically carried earnings to high levels. As a result, the earnings of many fishermen in New Bedford and Gloucester consistently exceeded those of manufacturing workers by multiples of two and three, suggesting compensation levels far above those needed to maintain the industry's labor supply.

The lay system also has an often overlooked effect upon profits and internal sources of funds for investment. By translating fluctuations in catch and price into swings in the earnings of fishermen, it also dampens swings in profits. During a downturn, immediate declines in wages help stabilize falling profits, thus deterring the exit of vessels. Likewise, during good times, short-term profits are siphoned off into wages, thereby diminishing incentives to new investment and the entry of vessels.

These two effects—the possibility of very high pay for fishermen under certain market conditions and the dampening of profit incentives—have different implications for kinship and capitalist vessels. When capitalist vessels are facing good times, for example, some of the increased revenue that would accrue to capital under more traditional pay arrangements is siphoned off into higher labor earnings.

On kinship vessels, however, the collective nature of the fishing enterprise blurs the distinction between profits and wages. During profitable times, higher wages increase, rather than detract from, the funds collectively available for new investment. During downturns, capital and labor on kinship vessels experience the same losses as capitalist vessels do, but they can continue to draw on collective sources of family capital to continue fishing. As a result, kinship vessels are better positioned for investment purposes than capitalist vessels. This asymmetrical effect of economic fluctuations on profits and investment funds helps to explain why kinship vessels have grown in importance during the unsettled 1970s and 1980s.

KINSHIP EMPLOYMENT SYSTEMS
AND ECONOMIC SECURITY

Just as the lay system is grounded in customs of income sharing, the practice of work sharing on kinship vessels can be partly traced to cultural and familial customs among first- and second-generation Italian and Portuguese fishermen. These emphasize traditions of family production and the collective responsibility of the whole family for the economic well-being of relatives.

Worksharing within kinship systems, however, also plays a contemporary economic role in providing important income, job security, and career opportunities for fishermen. For fishermen strongly attached to fishing as a way of life, kinship systems ensure continued access to preferred careers and guarantee a more stable (and often higher-paying) job than is available elsewhere in the local area. In addition, for poorly educated fishermen and for recent immigrants, kinship systems provide access to both income and a supportive work environment.

Little data are available on the quantitative importance of kinship employment systems in the two ports.[11] In Gloucester, however, where surveys have shown that the vast majority of vessels and almost all highliners are owned and operated by Italians, almost half of all fishermen are Italian and can be presumed to have some claim to kinship employment. In New Bedford, the dominant group participating in kinship employment arrangements is the Portuguese who constitute over a third of the commercial fishermen. Because almost all the scallop vessels and a majority of the finfishing boats are owned by non-Portuguese, however, many of these Portuguese are employed on capitalist vessels. Most scallop crews, in particular, lack the strong ethnic or family ties that characterize Italian groundfishing boats in Gloucester and Portuguese groundfishing boats in New Bedford.

On balance, capitalist arrangements are much more important in New Bedford than in Gloucester where kinship employment practices are more prevalent. Over time, however, the trend in finfishing in both ports has been for kinship employment systems to grow more important.

Employment Systems and Labor Relations

The distinction between capitalist and kinship employment systems in fishing is also reflected in the labor relations arrangements in the two systems. Although fishermen in both Gloucester and New Bedford are represented by trade unions, collective bargaining is a major factor in determining pay and job security only in New Bedford. Collective bargaining provides protections and safeguards for crew members who would otherwise be subject to the will of the employer. Formal contractual rules and a grievance procedure are relied upon to ensure fair treatment. Well over half the fishermen in New Bedford are members of the union, and it is strongest in scalloping where the capitalist employment systems are most prevalent.

In contrast, the fishermen's union in Gloucester, where kinship employment systems predominate, serves a social rather than economic purpose. The decline of the union as a major force in regulating wages and employment has roughly paralleled the increasing hegemony of Italian kinship employment systems. As the Gloucester fleet became dominated by Italians, the protections of kinship rules began to supplant employment systems governed by collective bargaining.[12] In the kinship sector, the rights and responsibilities of "family" are far more important safeguards than a union. As a result, there is more informality and flexibility in the rules of the employment systems. This even applies on kinship boats in New Bedford that are nominally covered by collective bargaining agreements.

Labor Market Structure and Adjustment to Economic Change

From the preceding discussion it should be obvious that there are two distinct patterns of labor market adjustment within the offshore fishing industry. The kinship sector, which consists of ethnically owned and operated vessels primarily engaged in groundfishing, is governed by strong ethnic employment commitments and follows worksharing principles. Because kinship vessels are family owned and operated, they tend not to discharge workers. Instead, they stabilize employment, both through worksharing and by continuing to operate vessels as long as variable costs are being covered. The capitalist sector exhibits a tendency to adjust crew size to the volume of catch, to make layoffs according to seniority, and to remove unprofitable boats from service.

In both sectors, however, income adjusts to economic change through "lay systems" that automatically link crew earnings to boat revenue. Changes in the volume of catch (holding the price of fish constant) are immediately translated into changes in income, especially in kinship systems where crew size is also maintained.

DIFFERENCES BETWEEN PORTS

In principle, the fishing sector could adjust to a permanent reduction in catch in a number of ways. Boats might operate with fewer crewmen and fresh-fish processing firms with fewer workers, thereby forcing the unemployed to absorb a disproportionate burden of the income loss. Where worksharing is used in lieu of layoffs, income per worker would fall as revenues declined. Finally, some boats or processing firms could cease to operate altogether, causing losses both for displaced workers and for private investors, family members, or banks that financed the vessels.

In practice, however, given that work and pay rules in both the kinship and the capitalist employment systems are relatively well defined and constant over time, the consequences of economic change for each type of employment system are remarkably predictable. Moreover, the pattern of adjustment will vary by port according to the mix between kinship and capitalist employment systems.

In Gloucester (where kinship employment systems are most influential) economic declines, for example, would first affect the marginal vessels in the port. Interviews indicate that marginal vessels tend to employ more non-Italians, suggesting that crew reductions of one or two would be likely on such boats. Thereafter, kinship commitments to employment and worksharing would tend to act as a buffer against further layoffs. The lay system, which guarantees coverage of variable boat expenses and which automatically adjusts labor costs to revenue declines, helps to make it economically possible for these kinship boats to maintain employment during adverse economic conditions.

Although kinship boats in Gloucester would continue to fish, they would not be unaffected by declines in catch. Many would experience sharply diminished profits. Boats would reduce crew size, but only an extreme decline in catch is likely to disrupt kinship commitments.

It seems evident that the fishermen with the least experience and the fewest family connections are most likely to experience unemployment in the face of adverse economic conditions in fishing. Those with extensive experience and strong ties with the Italian community are the last to face dismissal. The more likely outcome in Gloucester, therefore, is an increase in general underemployment rather than in unemployment.

Because capitalist employment systems are much more common in New Bedford, and because union regulation of employment is more important, adjustment to economic decline in that city would follow a somewhat different pattern from that of Gloucester. Adjustments on New Bedford finfishing vessels will be similar to those already described for Gloucester vessels. These boats typically engage a crew of five to seven members, and there is some room for down-sizing of the bigger crews. On those kinship vessels in the New Bedford fishing fleet, family members will be sheltered from layoffs. On nonunion vessels governed by capitalist employment practices, the less-skilled fishermen are most vulnerable to layoffs. On union boats, seniority governs layoffs, but because the more skilled are typically the first hired, those with fewer skills are most likely to become unemployed.

Employment on scallop vessels would be substantially affected by economic adversity. Scallop boats now employ crews of ten to thirteen, but the demands of the gear would permit reductions to as low as nine or ten on large boats. Given the technical feasibility of reducing scallop crews, and because there are few kinship ties to prevent crew reductions, employment loss is inevitable.

As mentioned earlier, the mix between kinship and capitalist vessels has been changing in both Gloucester and New Bedford. Gloucester's finfish fleet has become predominately an Italian kinship fleet in the past two decades. Similar trends are now occurring through the growth of Portuguese finfish vessels in New Bedford. Only scalloping remains primarily organized according to capitalist principles, although this is changing gradually, also. As a result, finfishing in these ports is less and less likely to show employment adjustment in the face of economic change.

Although this would suggest a growing rigidity in labor utilization in finfishing, there are important positive aspects of this development. The kinship sector acts as a safety net to fishermen who would otherwise be displaced during periods of economic downturn. This is particularly important for poorly educated and immigrant workers who are most likely to be handicapped in finding alternative employment. During periods of expansion, kinship systems tap into a unique labor reserve—an elastic supply of relatives willing to immigrate to the United States—which is skilled in fishing and committed to working hard in the industry.

A second source of rigidity in the employment systems in offshore fishing is related to entry barriers. In addition to substantive capital requirements for purchasing large vessels, the skill of the captain is critical to a vessel's earnings. This skill, however, can only be acquired by working alongside the captain, and such opportunities for training are zealously guarded. Kinship systems often encourage the passing of skills from father to son or from uncle to nephew, but such processes work slowly. As a result, skill bottlenecks can persist in offshore fishing which limit entry of additional vessels and raise vessel earnings. Because vessel earnings are translated into crew earnings through the lay system, fishermen with

Offshore stern trawler in Fairhaven.
Photo: National Marine Fisheries Service

relatively little formal education or training can earn the relatively high incomes observed in the industry.

Who Are the Marginal Fishermen?

The two patterns of labor market adjustment in fishing described above represent different "models" of the economic organization of the industry, each of which responds in a particular way to economic change and each of which contributes differently to the pool of dislocated workers following an adverse economic shock to the industry. It is the "least attached" workers who will be dislocated in all cases, but each part of the industry has a different definition of attachment. In the capitalist sector, attachment is defined by vessel seniority—those last hired on particular vessels will be the first to be laid off—on unionized vessels and by productivity on nonunion vessels. Labor adjustment can be fairly rapid, but the characteristics of workers displaced will vary between unionized and nonunionized vessels.

In the kinship sector, attachment is defined by a relationship to the family owning the vessel. Although there may be some workers in the kinship sector who have no kinship claim to continued employment, most workers are more or less permanently attached to the industry and to their family's vessels. Employment adjustment in the kinship sector is therefore relatively inflexible.

The imprint of these different systems can be seen in the characteristics of Massachusetts fishermen who actually experience job loss in the industry. From a sample of Massachusetts unemployed fishermen during 1981 and 1982, it is possible to determine some of the characteristics of fishermen most vulnerable to job loss.[13] While there are no data on the actual type of employment system under which these unemployed fishermen had previously worked, differences in the patterns of unemployment between the two ports are consistent with the observed differences in labor market institutions.

The key finding is that unemployed Gloucester fishermen tend to be older than those in New Bedford, despite the fact that the fishing labor force is younger than in New Bedford (see table 5–1). This finding is consistent with the practice of giving young fishermen on kinship vessels equal preference with adults for jobs and employment security. The concentration of unemployment among Gloucester fishermen over fifty-two

TABLE 5–1   *Age Distribution of Fishermen Claiming*
Unemployment Insurance, 1981–82

	Gloucester* N=43	New Bedford* N=69
Under 22	14.0%	15.9%
23–32	30.2	29.8
33–42	14.0	24.6
43–52	11.7	15.9
53+	30.2	14.4

*Totals do not come to 100 percent due to rounding.

Although these two distributions are only statistically different at the 75 percent level, they arise from work forces in the two ports that have distinctly different age distributions. For example, unpublished United States census data for 1980 show that less than 20 percent of the Gloucester fishermen were over forty-four, compared to almost 50 percent for New Bedford. As a result, fishermen over forty-four in Gloucester were more than twice as likely to be unemployed than would be indicated by their proportion of the fishing labor force. In New Bedford this relationship is reversed with older fishermen being one-third less likely to be unemployed. These differences in the proportions of older workers among the unemployed and the labor force are statistically significant at the 99 percent level in both Gloucester and New Bedford.

SOURCE: Unpublished sample survey, Massachusetts Division of Employment Security

years old further suggests that older family members may be relieved of full-time employment responsibilities, particularly during the arduous winter months. In New Bedford, however, unemployment is more heavily concentrated among younger fishermen, indicating the relatively greater importance of seniority in that port.

There are also substantial differences in the number of fishing vessels on which these unemployed fishermen had worked during the previous year. The Gloucester group reveals much stronger attachment to a single vessel than the New Bedford group. In Gloucester, over 60 percent of the fishermen had worked on a single boat, as would be expected in a kinship port, whereas in New Bedford only about one-third had worked on only one boat. Similarly, Gloucester has many fewer fishermen who worked for several employers than New Bedford. In New Bedford, almost half the unemployed sample worked for three or more employers during the year compared to about 13 percent for Gloucester.

According to information obtained from interviews, and in comparison to the average earnings of fishermen reported by the Massachusetts Division of Employment Security, the earnings of unemployed fishermen are considerably below those for fishermen in general. Median earnings during the previous year were between $12,000 and $14,000, compared to $18,285 for fishermen statewide. This finding applies equally to Gloucester and New Bedford. Both Gloucester and New Bedford, however, have relatively few unemployed fishermen earning under $6,000 whereas almost three-fourths of those in the rest of the state are in that category. This reinforces the finding that Gloucester and New Bedford are highliner, year-round ports. On the other hand, Gloucester has a higher proportion of its unemployed earning less than $18,000 (81.3 percent) compared to New Bedford (55.9 percent). Nearly one-quarter of New Bedford's unemployed fishermen earned over $24,000 compared to less than 10 percent for Gloucester (see table 5–2). As discussed previously, this difference between the ports is not surprising due to the much greater importance of scallops in the New Bedford catch.

TABLE 5–2 *Earnings Distribution of Fishermen Claiming Unemployment Insurance, 1981–82*

	Gloucester* N=43	New Bedford* N=69
Less than $6,000	16.2%	14.4%
$6,001–$12,000	30.2	22.7
$12,001–$18,000	34.9	18.8
$18,001–$24,000	9.3	20.3
$24,001+	9.3	24.6

*Totals do not come to 100 percent due to rounding. A X^2 test indicates a difference between the earnings distributions in the two ports that is statistically significant at approximately the 7 percent level.

SOURCE: Unpublished sample survey, Massachusetts Division of Employment Security

Although these findings provide some indication of the types of workers in both ports who are "marginal" and face the effects of routine fluctuations in the industry, they are not necessarily a reliable guide to how employment systems in fishing would react to more severe shocks. The rules of employment systems are likely to provide better predictions of such major changes. For example, a deep cut in scallop catch would presumably dislocate substantial numbers of older and more experienced Portuguese fishermen with substantially higher earnings than those currently unemployed, whereas similar reductions in finfishing would displace fewer workers (particularly in Gloucester) because of kinship protections.

Heavy seas.
Photo: National Marine Fisheries
Service

Other Adjustments in Fishing

Although the bulk of this chapter has focused on how employment systems affect patterns of layoff, worksharing, and income in fishing and processing, the distinction between kinship vessels and capitalist vessels carries over into other aspects of economic adjustment in fishing. For example, it could be argued that fishing is potentially a very "footloose" industry. A decline in catch in one port might well be handled by moving to other fishing grounds and other ports where fish are more abundant.

This occurs particularly in the inshore industry, but sometimes happens in the offshore sector as well. For example, New Bedford scallop boats have gone as far as the mid-Atlantic (off the New Jersey and Maryland coasts) to fish for scallops, although in recent times these areas have not yielded sufficient catches to warrant such long trips. An alternative for scallop fishermen would be intensified fishing—more trips or longer trips. However, this would have to overcome the union and custom-sanctified rules for length and frequency of fishing trips.

For finfish boats, intensified fishing schedules do not offer a ready means of compensating for the increased competition or output losses in particular fishing grounds. Boats already spend as much time at sea as possible, and attempts to lengthen this time would mean remaining at sea under adverse weather conditions, increased risk, and would reduce the freshness of catch.

The other alternative, temporary or permanent movement of fishing vessels to ports elsewhere in the country, is also possible, but this is not likely to be a frequent occurrence. Our interviews showed that kinship vessels have strong ties to their families and to the ethnic communities of their ports, and these inhibit the transfer of fishing operations, even in the worst of times. Among capitalist vessels as well, captains and owners seem to have strong attachments to their particular ports and are not likely to migrate readily.

Because attachment to "home" ports, particularly among family-owned boats, is a strong deterrent to mobility, kinship employment systems would seem to be particularly vulnerable to "forced" exit through bankruptcy in the case of a decline in earnings. But the same kinship systems that provide a network of job guarantees also provide resources for boat financing. For example, the lay system used in family vessels in Gloucester earmarks a larger fraction of catch revenues for the boat than is true on capitalist vessels in New Bedford. Moreover, collateral for bank loans and repayment responsibilities can be widely pooled within kinship systems, making credit easier to obtain and loans easier to pay back.

Employment Systems and Labor Market Adjustment in Processing

In contrast to fishing, the employment systems in fish processing in both ports are almost entirely organized along conventional capitalist industrial lines. Employment varies according to seasonal and longer-term changes in the availability of fish. Compensation arrangements for production workers in processing are generally fixed on an hourly basis for periods of a year. Wages are unaffected by short-term changes in the volume or price of catch.

Despite the overall similarities in the employment and pay systems in fish processing in both ports, there are important distinctions in the way in which these systems handle seasonal fluctuations in the demand for fresh-fish processing. In New Bedford, which has somewhat less seasonality in catch than Gloucester, demand fluctuations are met largely through variations in hours worked. In Gloucester, however, there is a much heavier reliance upon expanding and contracting employment of the casual labor pool.

Fish processing in New Bedford is handled by a core of adult workers who are regularly employed year round. Peak demand during the summer is met partly by hiring additional adult females, but the length of the work day for the core work group is also increased substantially so that a certain amount of worksharing is involved.

There is also a core of adult, year-round workers in Gloucester. This group, however, is smaller than in New Bedford and is supplemented by a second, also smaller, group of regularly employed part-year workers— adults who work during the spring, summer, and early fall. These part-year workers are often employed long enough for them to qualify for unemployment insurance benefits during the winter months. Finally, peak demand in Gloucester is met through the employment of a large group of younger workers—high school and college students—who roughly double the size of the processing labor force during the summer months. Thus, even within capitalist employment systems, there can be variations in employment strategies.

A decline in catch would lead to different employment impacts in fresh- and frozen-fish processing. Frozen-fish processors, who depend almost entirely on foreign imports, would be immune to any local change in catch. Because they employ the bulk of the processing labor force in Gloucester (approximately 80 percent), processing as a whole in Gloucester would be far less affected than in New Bedford, where frozen-fish processing is minimal.

The fresh-fish processors, by contrast, would be affected more seriously by a decline in local fishing. If the decline affected only one species, offsetting adjustments might be made by switching to other species. Widespread declines in catch, however, would be immediately translated into reduced employment because processing is organized along capitalist employment practices.

In Gloucester, most processors would retain their core crew of year-round workers, and would also try to retain the supplemental regular crew of seasonal workers who return every peak season. Gloucester processors, however, operate with a large pool of casual summer workers. These workers, mostly students, would be highly vulnerable to employment loss.

Unlike Gloucester, New Bedford relies heavily upon a stable, year-round, fresh-fish processing work force whose hours of work are adjusted to changes in the volume of catch. Thus, contractions in the average work week would be the principal avenue of adjustment, although some reductions in employment would also occur. Because so little onshore labor is required to process scallops, declines in the scallop catch would have only a small effect overall on either employment or pay in the processing work force.

Summary

Central to understanding the adjustment processes within the fishing industry is a knowledge of the workplace "employment systems" in fishing and processing. The rules in both kinship and capitalist employment systems allow for flexibility in resources during periods of growth, as local labor supplies are relatively elastic and can be augmented by new immigration of Italians and Portuguese. In periods of decline, however, the kinship employment systems operate to cushion the impact of decline, to sustain the attachment of the work force to fishing careers, and to moderate processes for resource mobility.

Given the institutional rules that divide offshore fishing into kinship and capitalist sectors and that govern pay and employment in processing, it is possible to trace the various paths of adjustment in employment and income within the fishing industries of Gloucester and New Bedford. Reductions in catch at constant prices would lead to diminished income on all vessels; reductions in employment would be confined largely to capitalist vessels; and there would perhaps be some bankruptcy of marginal, capitalist vessels.

In Gloucester, fishermen with the least experience, those few on marginal capitalist vessels, and those with the weakest connections to the Sicilian fishing families would be most subject to unemployment. In New Bedford, similar considerations would affect adjustment patterns in finfishing. On scallop vessels, there would be reductions in crew size, generally following union seniority rules, and some scallop boats might cease operation.

Kinship vessels have been growing in importance in relation to capitalist vessels in finfishing. Over time, this means that the employment rigidities, the economic buffers, and the labor expansion potential associated with kinship employment systems are increasingly shaping income, employment, and adjustment processes in finfishing. Capitalist adjustments, however, remain the rule in scalloping.

Because fresh-fish processing in both Gloucester and New Bedford is organized around capitalist employment systems, employment in both ports would be affected by a decline in catch. Nevertheless, there are differences between the two ports. Summer and part-year jobs would bear the brunt of the employment loss in Gloucester, whereas the full-time work force would face reduced hours in New Bedford. Frozen-fish processors in Gloucester would be relatively unaffected by changes in local catch because they depend on foreign imports.

Because the fishing sector in Gloucester is buffered against the employment consequences of adverse changes in catch by kinship employment systems in fishing, by the presence of frozen-fish processors that do not rely on local catch, and by the use of students in fresh-fish processing in the summer, the core work force in the fishing sector is likely to remain employed during periods of economic decline. New Bedford, however, lacks these buffers. As a result, the employment effects of an adverse change in catch will be more severe in New Bedford than in Gloucester. Both ports, however, will experience a loss in income unless there are off-setting changes in fish prices.

For the individuals affected by economic change, the crucial question is the ease with which they can transfer into alternative employment. This will depend upon the skills of displaced workers, the absorptive capacity of the port economies, and the earning potential from alternative jobs. These issues are addressed in the next chapter.

SIX

*Employment and Income Alternatives
to Fishing and Processing*

The fishing industry is subject to frequent shocks and fluctuations, some of which are quite severe. These shocks are then transmitted through various types of employment and pay systems that produce different patterns of adjustment in employment and income within the industry. To continue the theme of adjustment, it is necessary to explore the prospects for finding alternative jobs elsewhere in the economy if workers are displaced by a downturn in the fishing industry.

Adjustments involving the larger economy depend both upon which workers (in terms of their skills and experience) are displaced from the fishing sector and upon the skill requirements and availability of jobs outside fishing. The former are determined by the operation of the employment systems in the fishing industry, and the latter by the structure and prosperity of the surrounding economy. Because labor migrates, the adjustment process ordinarily would be considered in a wider context than that of a local labor market. However, a wide variety of interview data shows that economic and kinship factors strongly tie most workers in the fishing industry to their communities and therefore adjustment processes tend to be unusually localized. This chapter will examine skill transferability and labor absorption in the context of the Gloucester and New Bedford labor markets.

A review of the structure and trends in the two local economies will provide a general background for understanding the different absorptive environments that displaced workers face in the two ports. It is then necessary to compare the skills and experience of workers most likely to be displaced from various segments of the industry—kinship vessels, capitalist vessels, and fresh-fish processing plants—with detailed information on the skill requirements and earnings of alternative jobs in each port and to study the role of income transfers in cushioning labor market adjustments.

The Economies of Gloucester and New Bedford

CURRENT STATUS

The economies of Gloucester and New Bedford have little in common other than a relatively high dependence upon fishing. The city of Gloucester's population (27,717 in 1980) is a little over one-quarter the size of the city of New Bedford's (98,478 in 1980).[1] New Bedford is part of an SMSA that had a population of 169,425 in 1980, whereas Gloucester and its surrounding towns had a population of only around 40,000 in 1980.

Gloucester is a wealthier community than New Bedford. Median family income in 1979 in the city of New Bedford was $14,930 and in the SMSA, $16,915, compared to $19,213 for Gloucester and $21,166 for the state. Over 14 percent of the city of New Bedford families had income below the poverty line (10.6 percent in the SMSA) compared to 8.8 percent for Gloucester and 7.6 percent for the state.

The median level of education of persons twenty-five years old and older in the city of New Bedford, 9.5 years in 1980, is considerably lower than that in the city of Gloucester (12.4 years) and the state (12.6 years). In 1980 over 60 percent of those twenty-five years old and older in the city of New Bedford had not graduated from high school, compared to about one-third in the city of Gloucester and 27.8 percent in Massachusetts overall; almost half of the population twenty-five years old and older in New Bedford had eight or fewer years of formal education relative to about 15 percent in both the city of Gloucester and statewide.

In terms of industrial structure, a higher percentage of New Bedford's employment is in manufacturing than in Gloucester, and almost a third of this is concentrated in low-wage jobs in highly competitive industries such as apparel and textiles (see tables 6–1 and 6–2).[2] Such low-wage employment is consistent with the relatively low levels of education in the work force and both contribute to the economic poverty of the area.

The concentration of low-wage industries in New Bedford's manufacturing base is also evident from average annual earnings data (see table 6–3). In 1980 average annual earnings in manufacturing were 23 percent below the Gloucester average and 26 percent below the statewide average.

Although Gloucester and New Bedford provide lower-paying work,

TABLE 6–1   Private Sector Employment in the New Bedford L M A *by Industry*

	1980 Employment	% of private employment	Average annual percent change	
			1970–75	1975–80
Agriculture, forestry, fisheries	2,231	4.0%	− 2.0	+ 12.3
Mining*	——	——	− 2.2	——
Construction	1,581	2.8	− 5.5	+ 1.8
Manufacturing	25,407	45.7	− 3.8	+ 3.5
Durable goods	8,296	14.9	− 6.8	+ 8.9
Furniture, lumber, wood products	288	0.5	− 9.4	+ 7.3
Primary metals	1,105	2.0	+ 4.9	− 1.8
Fabricated metals	1,835	3.3	− 9.0	+ 9.5
Nonelectric machinery	1,085	2.0	− 12.1	+22.9
Electric machinery	2,421	4.4	− 9.7	+ 9.8
Transportation equipment	597	1.1	− 8.5	+19.8
Instruments	965	1.7	+353.7	+10.4
Other*	——	——	− 16.8	——
Nondurable goods	17,111	30.8	− 2.4	+ 1.5
Food, kindred	1,821	3.3	− 4.5	+ 7.6
Textile mill products	2,289	4.1	− 7.6	+ 3.8
Apparel, fabricated textiles	8,259	14.9	− 1.2	+ 1.9
Printing, publishing	732	1.3	+ 0.8	+ 1.3
Chemical and allied products	158	0.3	+ 14.8	+ 2.4
Rubber	1,261	2.3	− 5.8	− 4.8
Other.	2,591	4.7	+ 4.6	− 0.1
Transportation, communications, utilities	1,930	3.5	+ 2.9	− 5.2
Wholesale and retail trade	12,540	22.6	+ 1.6	+ 0.6
Finance, insurance, real estate	1,936	3.5	+ 3.2	+ 3.1
Services	9,054	16.3	+ 12.8	+ 3.1
Total private employment[a]	55,558	100.0	− 0.5	+ 2.8

* 1980 employment figures were not released for reasons of confidentiality, but are included in the totals.

[a] Includes mining employment and some employment that was not classified in any industry.

S O U R C E : Research Department, Massachusetts Division of Employment Security; "Massachusetts Department of Manpower Development, Labor Market Information, Planning Package, Fiscal Year 1983, New Bedford CETA Consortium," April 1982, pp. IV 3–4.

TABLE 6–2   Private Sector Employment in the Gloucester LMA by Industry

	1980 Employment	% of private employment	Average annual percent change 1970–75	1975–80
Agriculture, forestry, fisheries	990	7.6	− 1.4	+ 8.9
Mining	0	0.0	0.0	0.0
Construction	430	3.3	− 1.4	+ 1.8
Manufacturing	4,766	36.8	+ 6.2	+ 7.9
Durable goods	2,259	17.4	+ 32.6	+15.7
Furniture, lumber, wood products	8	0.1	− 3.6	− 2.2
Primary metals	70	0.5	− 12.3	+11.8
Fabricated metals	268	2.1	+ 54.4	+ 2.1
Nonelectric machinery	938	7.2	+106.3	+ 9.1
Electric machinery	537 [a]	4.1 [b]	+ 93.8	+98.0 [c]
Transportation equipment	90	0.7	+ 3.6	− 9.3
Instruments	10 [a]	0.1 [b]	0.0	0.0
Other	10 [a]	0.1 [b]	+ 9.1	− 17.3 [c]
Nondurable goods	2,507	19.4	+ 0.5	+ 3.3
Food, kindred	1,510	11.7	+ 3.9	+ 1.7
Textile mill products	15 [a]	0.1 [b]	+ 4.6	− 1.3 [c]
Apparel, fabricated textiles	212 [a]	1.6 [b]	− 2.7	− 1.8 [c]
Printing, publishing	333	2.6	+ 17.4	− .5
Chemical and allied products	9 [a]	0.1 [b]	− 15.4	0.0 [c]
Rubber	1 [a]	0.0 [b]	− 19.9	− 10.0 [c]
Other	231 [a]	1.8 [b]	+ 3.8	+11.0 [c]
Transportation, communications, utilities	587	4.5	+ 14.3	+12.2
Wholesale and retail trade	3,650	28.2	+ 2.6	+ 4.9
Finance, insurance, real estate	355	2.7	+ 3.4	+ 4.1
Services	2,174	16.8	+ 20.2	+ 4.8
Total private employment	12,952	99.9	+ 5.5	+ 6.0

[a] This is 1978 employment, as 1980 employment was not released to protect individual firm confidentiality.

[b] This is 1978 employment as a percent of total 1980 private employment.

[c] This is average annual percent change, 1975–1978.

SOURCE: Massachusetts Division of Employment Security

TABLE 6–3   *Average Annual Earnings by Industry, 1980*

	New Bedford	Gloucester	Massachusetts
Agriculture, forestry, fisheries	$17,242	$15,108	$11,775
Construction	13,693	12,618	16,811
Manufacturing	12,082	15,693	16,436
Transportation, communications, utilities	16,872	14,792	18,725
Wholesale and retail trade*	11,038	10,973	10,165
Finance, insurance, real estate	11,106	12,265	15,247
Services	9,804	8,022	11,904
All industries	11,858	12,810	13,815

*Also includes government
SOURCE: Massachusetts Division of Employment Security

on average, than the state as a whole, the pattern is reversed in the broad category "agricultural, forestry, and fisheries," which is dominated by relatively high-wage fishing in both communities. High earnings in fishing are especially evident in New Bedford because scallops and yellowtail flounder, which represent a large percentage of the New Bedford catch, are of much higher value than the cod and haddock that comprise most of the Gloucester catch.

CYCLICAL PERFORMANCE AND PAST TRENDS

The current state of both economies gives only a partial picture of their ability to absorb displaced workers. For a more complete picture, it is necessary to examine employment trends to discover whether alternative occupations are in sectors that are likely to be expanding in the future or that are likely to remain stable or decline.

Both Gloucester and New Bedford have had persistent unemployment in excess of the statewide levels. From 1975 to 1980 the unemployment rate for the New Bedford Labor Market Area (LMA) followed a pattern similar to that of the state, declining yearly from 1975 to 1979, then increasing in 1980 (see table 6–4).[3] The level of unemployment during this period, however, was on average 2.8 percentage points higher in the New Bedford area than in the state overall. The unemployment rate in the Gloucester LMA declined gradually between 1975 and 1980, but it also remained higher than the state average throughout the period.

FIGURE 6–1   *Private Sector Employment in the New Bedford*
LMA, *the Gloucester* LMA, *and Massachusetts, 1970–1980*

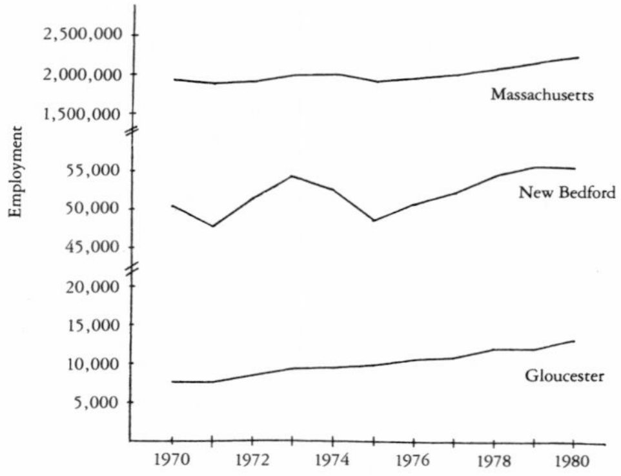

SOURCE: Massachusetts Division of Employment Security

Yearly data for the 1970s indicate that New Bedford's employment was much more cyclical than employment in Gloucester and the state (see fig. 6–1). New Bedford was particularly hard hit by the recession in the mid-1970s, with employment falling over 10 percent between 1973 and 1975, compared to a decline of 3.7 percent in Massachusetts and stable employment for Gloucester. Initially (1975–76), the New Bedford economy recovered from the recession faster than the state did, but from 1976 through 1979 its rate of growth began to lag behind that of the state, and in 1980 New Bedford again experienced employment declines. In comparison, Gloucester was more recession resistant. During the mid-1970s, for instance, although the rate of employment growth slowed, the level of employment did not fall as it did in New Bedford and the state.

During the first half of the 1970s, employment in manufacturing fell in New Bedford. Nondurable goods are the mainstay of New Bedford's manufacturing economy, so that, although employment in durable-goods manufacturing declined faster than that in nondurable manufacturing during the early 1970s, total job loss in nondurables was far greater. Nonmanufacturing employment in New Bedford continued to rise, led by significant growth in services, particularly in health fields.

In the latter half of the 1970s, manufacturing employment in New Bedford grew faster than employment in the local economy and was responsible for 35 percent of the job expansion from 1975 to 1980.

TABLE 6–4   *Unemployment Rates for New Bedford, Gloucester, and*
Massachusetts, 1975–1980

	New Bedford LMA	Gloucester LMA	Massachusetts
1975	14.0%	12.0%	11.2%
1976	11.4	10.7	9.5
1977	10.9	10.5	8.1
1978	8.5	9.8	6.1
1979	7.5	8.5	5.5
1980	8.1	8.2	5.6

SOURCE: Massachusetts Division of Employment Security, *Annual
Planning Information Report, Fiscal Year 1982, Massachusetts*, p. 69.

Although durable-goods manufacturing employed less than half the
number of workers in the nondurable-goods sector, the durable-goods industries accounted for two-thirds of the new manufacturing jobs during
this period. The bulk of these new jobs were in the electrical machinery,
instruments, and transportation (mostly shipbuilding and repairs) industries. In sharp contrast to the early 1970s, employment in the agriculture, forestry, and fisheries sector and in the food-manufacturing sector
(which includes fish processing) expanded by over 50 percent between
1975 and 1980. From 1978 to 1980 these two sectors alone accounted for
two-thirds of the new jobs in the New Bedford economy.

In Gloucester, employment in nondurable-goods manufacturing expanded slightly during the early 1970s. This was largely due to frozen-
fish processing, which maintained fairly steady employment during this
period. Also, in contrast to New Bedford, employment in Gloucester's
durable-goods manufacturing expanded dramatically during the 1970s.
High annual growth rates in nonelectrical machinery, electrical machinery, and fabricated metals helped to more than double the share of
employment in durable-goods manufacturing from 5.9 percent to 13.8
percent between 1970 and 1975. Growth in these three industries accounted for more than one-third (37 percent) of the new jobs in the
Gloucester LMA over the five-year period. As in New Bedford, the service sector in Gloucester experienced high growth, more than doubling
in size between 1970 and 1975.

In the latter half of the 1970s, average annual growth rates in Gloucester surpassed those of the earlier years and the shift toward durable-goods
manufacturing continued. Employment data through 1980 show the

FIGURE 6–2   *Gloucester* LMA, *Total and Selected Industries by Month, 1976–1980*

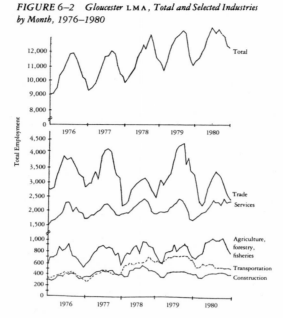

SOURCE: Massachusetts Division of Employment Security

durable-goods sector gaining momentum with "high-technology" firms leading the way. In contrast to New Bedford, employment in the trade and utilities sectors continued expanding rapidly during this period.

The generally stable, upward trend in employment, however, conceals considerable seasonality in the Gloucester labor market (see fig. 6–2). Tourism, primarily a spring and summer phenomenon, generates large increases in employment in trade and services in jobs that disappear in the fall and winter. The fishing and construction industries also expand substantially during the spring and summer only to contract again during the winter months. It is not unusual for employment in the summer months to be 25 percent higher than in the winter. In contrast, the New Bedford economy shows far less seasonality (see figs. 6–3 and 6–4).

FUTURE PROSPECTS

Both communities are projected to experience more than a 1 percent decline in population over the next decade, compared to a projected 2 percent increase statewide.[4] Economic projections for Glouces-

FIGURE 6–3   *Private Sector Employment in the New Bedford* L M A,
Selected Industries by Month, 1976–1980

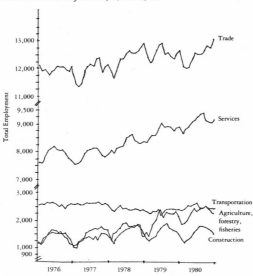

S O U R C E : Massachusetts Division of Employment Security

ter and New Bedford point to a continuation of past trends.[5] The instruments industry in New Bedford and the electrical-machinery and defense-related fabricated-metals industries in Gloucester made substantial contributions to employment expansion in the two communities in the late 1970s.

Although these growth industries have made large contributions to new job creation in the latter part of the 1970s, they still account for relatively small shares of total employment in both areas. The projections for growth in such "high-technology" industries are notoriously uncertain, but it seems unlikely that the growth rates of the 1970s can be sustained.[6] Since 1980, as a result of the recession, growth in many high-technology firms in the state has slackened, sometimes resulting in substantial layoffs. The only other major source of new jobs in these two labor markets in the recent past has been fishing and related industries.

It thus appears that, at least in the near future, these economies will have to rely on their largest, traditional employers: apparel and textile manufacturing in New Bedford and tourism (trade and services) in

FIGURE 6–4   *Private Sector Employment in the New Bedford* LMA, *by Month, 1976–1980*

SOURCE: Massachusetts Division of Employment Security

Gloucester. For New Bedford, this means dependence on generally low-wage industries that are vulnerable to both foreign competition and recession. Thus, New Bedford is likely to remain a precarious economy, providing predominately low-wage employment and suffering from recurrent periods of high unemployment. Gloucester's economic prospects are stronger, based on what happened in the 1970s, but they depend on the city's ability to sustain its record of growth in nondurable-goods manufacturing. Seasonality of employment, however, will continue to be a major feature of the Gloucester economy and will keep its unemployment rates higher than would otherwise be expected.

Reabsorbing Displaced Workers

Given the economic structures of the two ports, their patterns of cyclical and seasonal fluctuations in labor demand, and their future prospects, what can be said about the capacity of these local economies to cushion the impact of adverse economic change in the fishing industry? Although Gloucester has a somewhat stronger economy than New Bedford, the capacity of both economies to absorb displaced workers is highly dependent upon the national business cycle. If fishing-industry workers were displaced during a period of recession, few vacancies would exist and a backlog of laid-off workers would have to be recalled in many industries before there would be any new hiring. In periods of prosperity, job vacancies would be more plentiful, particularly those that are relatively low skilled.

The ease with which workers can transfer between the fishing sector and other parts of the economy depends partly upon the match between the skills of the fishing labor force and the requirements of jobs. It also depends upon the willingness of fishing-sector workers to accept employment in different industries and upon their attachment to the industry and their communities.

Earlier chapters have emphasized the commitment of many fishermen to their life-style at sea and the bonds of kinship and family that tie many of them to their local port communities. These ties to the fishing industry and community are further reinforced by the economic incentives of high earnings, employment guarantees, and lack of transferable education and skills. Attachment is strongest among ethnic fishermen working on family-operated offshore vessels. It is weakest among fishermen without ethnic connections and among those who work part time, often on smaller, inshore vessels.

These differences in attachment lead to the distinction, described in the previous chapter, between marginal and core fishermen. Some fishermen are marginally attached to the industry, either because fishing is not their sole source of income or because they lack employment protections from kinship or seniority. For core fishermen, fishing is a year-round occupation and their jobs are more secure as a result of kinship connections or seniority rights. Marginal workers are likely to be displaced by small fluctuations in the industry, whereas core workers will only be displaced by major disruptions. Marginal and core workers also differ in terms of their skills, work experience, and earnings capacity. These differences, in turn, influence the probability of each group's being successfully reabsorbed in their local port economies.

REEMPLOYING THE MARGINAL FISHERMEN

Both the interviews and the data on the characteristics of the unemployed reported in the previous chapter support the view that the fishermen most vulnerable to displacement are likely to be marginally attached to fishing and to receive wages below the average for the fishing industry. For most of the fishermen, both the Gloucester and New Bedford economies could provide alternative employment in high-technology firms and industries such as machine parts or apparel, at least during periods of relative prosperity. Such employment is likely to be more permanent in Gloucester because of the presence of a reasonably large number of firms that employ low-skilled workers in relatively stable jobs at wages roughly comparable to those earned by the majority of marginal fishermen. In the lower wage, more cyclical New Bedford economy, alternative employment is less certain.

This judgment is reinforced by interviews conducted with a large number of employers in both cities who were asked about their hiring policies, wage levels, skill requirements, and previous experience in hiring people associated with the fishing industry. For example, one firm in Gloucester manufactures electrical components. Out of a work force of 700, about 250 are in unskilled entry-level jobs, mostly in the stockroom and on the assembly floor. The wage scale starts at \$3.93 per hour and moves rapidly to \$5.60. Most stockroom workers earn between \$4.69 and \$6.17 per hour and most assemblers, between \$5.46 and \$7.22. The firm hires frequently from high-school vocational programs, but also hires older women and men. Another firm produces machine parts and employs 350 workers. Of these, 100 are assemblers, 150 are machine operators and machinists, and the rest are stockroom workers, packers, and the like. All the production workers are men. The firm pays between \$4.72 and \$9.99 an hour and has hired people from fishing-related backgrounds.

Additional evidence of the type of jobs available to marginal fishermen comes from the employment service job listings in Gloucester. In the past, most of these listings have been in the services, structural (skilled craftwork and unskilled general labor), and clerical areas. In 1980, average hourly wages for these jobs were \$3.15 in services, \$3.56 in clerical, and \$4.25 in structural positions. At that time, these wages were ten to fifty cents per hour lower than those for comparable jobs listed throughout the state.

Several conclusions emerge from examining these local companies and local job-vacancy data. First, the Gloucester economy experiences business cycles in much the same way as the rest of the nation. Thus, many of the firms outside the fishing sector that were surveyed as possible sources of alternative employment for fishing-sector workers would be able to hire new workers during prosperous periods, but not during economic downturns. At the time of the interviews, most firms had recently laid off workers, and these workers would have to be recalled before new hiring could take place. However, given normal attrition and prospects for long-term growth, there appeared to be reasonable prospects for an adequate number of job openings as the economy improved. Although the starting pay and average hourly pay of most of these firms is far below what the average fisherman earns, it is quite close to the median earnings reported by the sample of unemployed fishermen discussed in the previous chapter.

In New Bedford, as in Gloucester, a depressed national economy would make absorption of fishermen difficult. This would be compounded by the fact that average pay in New Bedford, even when work is available, is below that in Gloucester. Nevertheless, although the New Bedford economy has suffered more severe recessions than the Gloucester economy, there is evidence that there is employment available that is suitable for marginal fishermen. In particular, several apparel and textile firms have a labor force similar to this group of fishermen. A typical example is a firm that manufactures specialized fabrics and normally employs around 800 people. Because of slack economic conditions at the time of our interviews, 500 people were laid off. Average straight-time earnings are $5.50 per hour and the normal work week is forty-six hours, six of which are overtime.

In firms such as these, many of the workers are non-English speaking and of recent Portuguese origin. A job in these firms is often the first job an immigrant finds in New Bedford. These firms also have strong ties to the fishing community, and these would facilitate employment. Many of the employees have relatives connected to fishing, and some workers are saving to acquire a fishing boat, or intend to move into fishing as space on a family boat opens up. Although there appears to be little movement in reverse, i.e., from fishing to employment in such firms, there seem to be no barriers to employing displaced fishermen.

Unlike the situation in Gloucester, however, these firms are likely to be unstable and seasonal. As a result, people forced to move from fishing to the garment or textile industry may be worse off, depending on the stability of their previous employment on marginal boats. This is consistent with the fact that the business interviews uncovered very little evidence of mobility from fishing to garment or textile work.

The employment service job listings in New Bedford show that almost half the job orders placed between October 1980 and March 1981 were in the manufacturing sector. The bulk of the remaining openings were in wholesale and retail trade, public administration, and services. The occupational distribution of these jobs is given in table 6–5. Packaging and material handling, clerical, bench work (mostly assembly line), and sales jobs predominate. Average hourly wages for those jobs range from $3.31 in sales to $3.94 in packaging and handling. Structural occupations, processing occupations, and machine-trade occupations represented fewer vacancies but higher hourly wages ($4.18 to $5.18). Table 6–5 also shows that there were several applicants for most job openings.

Therefore, both economies have some capacity to reemploy displaced marginal fishermen. Employment in Gloucester seems more promising than in New Bedford given the healthier and higher-wage Gloucester economy. However, even though jobs with suitable pay are available to these fishermen, many may not be willing to accept the more regimented routine of factory work.

ADJUSTMENT TO DEEPER JOB CUTS
IN FISHING

Although many of the fishermen who are most vulnerable to displacement could find alternative employment in Gloucester and New Bedford, the next tier of fishermen to be displaced would be those on capitalist vessels who are more firmly attached to more prosperous boats or fishermen in the kinship sector with relatively distant family ties or low skills. These fishermen would be hard to relocate in comparable work. Most of the available jobs would entail a substantial reduction in earnings. Hourly earnings of the average fisherman are twice the earnings available in the manufacturing jobs for which they would be qualified.

A few firms in the Gloucester area offer a limited number of jobs that more closely match the wages of fishing, but these jobs tend to require skills that fishermen do not have. For example, one metal-working firm employs skilled lathe operators, forgers, and pressmen in a plant that has an average wage of about nine dollars an hour. This is below that earned by fully employed fishermen, but it might be argued that the safer and steadier work would compensate for the higher earnings in fishing. However, the requirements for these jobs place them out of reach of most fishermen. This observation is supported by the earlier finding that fish-

TABLE 6–5   *Job Orders Placed with the New Bedford Division of Employment Security, by Occupation**

Occupation openings	Number of openings	% of total openings	Average hourly wage**	Ratio of applicants to jobs
Professional, technical, management	77	4.4	5.96	6:1
Clerical	272	15.6	3.63	3:1
Sales	222	12.7	3.31	1:1
Services	165	9.4	3.37	6:1
Farm	45	2.6	3.40	2:1
Processing	28	1.6	4.71	5:1
Machine trades	156	8.9	5.18	2:1
Bench work	230	13.2	3.47	2:1
Structural occupations	118	6.7	4.18	4:1
Motor freight, transportation	155	8.9	3.41	1:1
Packaging, material handling	273	15.6	3.94	3:1
Other	8	0.5	4.84	3:1
Total	1,749	100.0	$3.89	3:1

*October 1, 1980 to March 31, 1981
**As of April 30, 1981
SOURCE: Massachusetts Division of Employment Security, *Annual Planning Information Report, Fiscal Year 1982, New Bedford* LMA, pp. 32–34.

ermen, as a group, lack the previous work experience and education necessary for comparably paying shore positions.

The major high-wage employers in New Bedford are in the durable goods sector, but many of these firms are in a long-term decline because of the difficulties in the auto industry. Another plausible alternative is construction, but this industry is also experiencing a cyclical decline and its long-term growth prospects are poor. A further possibility is the electrical firms that have located in the New Bedford area. The interviews indicated that these firms expect to expand their employment with the end of the recession, but that they seek people for assembly and semi-skilled wire-working occupations. About half these jobs are held by men and the starting salary is just below $4.00 an hour. After one or two years the pay rises to $7.00 per hour. Thus, these firms do not seem to provide adequate substitute jobs for unemployed fishermen.

Therefore, although both economies could absorb fishermen with low earnings who are loosely attached to the industry, absorption of the majority of fishermen would be quite difficult. In addition to the dramatic change in working conditions, most alternative employment either involves substantial wage declines or demands skills that are significantly different from those in fishing. Moreover, most of the new employment available to fishermen in the New Bedford area is in declining, highly cyclical manufacturing industries that do not provide stable employment prospects for entry-level employees.

Absorption of Processing Workers

Processing is governed entirely by capitalist employment systems. As a result, economic decline is translated directly into reductions in labor demand. Processing workers have few skills other than manual dexterity and an ability to work long hours under often unpleasant conditions. In New Bedford, disadvantages of low skill are compounded by a lack of fluency in English.

The regular fresh-fish processing employees in both cities exhibit a strong attachment to specific firms. As noted in chapter 4, the average age of this group is high and the most recent pay scales range between $6.50 and $7.00 an hour. A typical medium-sized firm would have ten to twelve cutters (mostly men), forty to fifty packers (mostly women), and ten general laborers (mostly men). It is not clear which group of these full-time workers would be the first to be laid off, but there were some hints in the interviews that cutters might be vulnerable because they are the least willing to do other kinds of work within the plant and because they can be replaced by automatic filleting machines.

Despite these common elements, adjustment patterns differ significantly between Gloucester and New Bedford. In Gloucester there are three major groups of fresh-fish processing employees: full-year, full-time adults; part-year, full-time adults regularly hired each summer; and college and high-school students who are more casually hired for the summer. New Bedford processors hire very few students and rely more heavily on full-time workers whose work hours are varied with changing demand.

In the event of a reduction in processing employment in Gloucester, the first group to be laid off would be the students. These young workers would probably be able to find employment in the local tourist industry and thus the loss of employment would not pose a great hardship for them. In New Bedford, hours worked by full-time adults would contract, but the level of employment would not immediately fall.

If full-time fresh-fish workers in either city lost their jobs, they would only be able to find new jobs that made direct use of their skills in frozen-fish processing. However, this sector has not been hiring in recent years so reemployment is unlikely. In general, displaced processing workers would be eligible for the same types of jobs described above as possible employment alternatives for fishermen. In fact, many of these jobs are more suitable for processors than for fishermen. Working conditions are similar, and starting pay and average hourly pay, although below that for processing, are universally closer to processors' earnings than to fishermen's earnings.

In particular, a marine equipment manufacturer in Gloucester employs two hundred workers, of whom about 50 percent are unskilled. Of the unskilled employees, about 85 percent are women, many of whom have previously worked in processing. The pay range is $5.75 to $6.50 an hour. In New Bedford, a firm producing capacitors for electrical appliances employs 600 workers, and is planning to expand with the end of the recession. Most of the jobs involve semiskilled wrapping of coils. Starting wages are $3.84 an hour and rise to $7.00 with a few years of experience. The labor force is almost half male and fairly young. The most recently hired workers do not have high-school diplomas, and a small fraction of the work force does not speak English. The firm does not like to hire fishermen, but has hired many workers from fish processing and presumably would do so again.

Although these wages are lower than current processing workers' earnings, it is important to remember that processing work is seasonal and many processing workers are laid off in the winter. As a result, their annual income, even with unemployment benefits, is below that implied by simple comparisons of hourly earnings in processing with those in other industries.

Again, most firms indicated they would have to rehire those workers laid off by the recent recession before hiring processors. Also, alternative employment in New Bedford is not as attractive as that available in Gloucester, due to its high potential for cyclical layoffs and eventual permanent unemployment. Nonetheless, there is considerable alternative employment and many employers indicated during interviews that they would regard processing workers as a good potential labor force.

In general, apart from overall shortages of jobs in the two economies, neither problems of skill transferability nor economic disincentives will impede the transfer of displaced processing workers into other low-wage entry jobs in both communities. In Gloucester, the seasonal nature of processing employment fits nicely with the seasonality of tourism. The seasonality of workers and jobs facilitates absorption of displaced processing workers and cushions the vulnerability of full-time workers to displacement. In New Bedford, displaced processing workers would largely require full-time alternative jobs.

Unemployment Insurance and Other Income Transfers

To the extent that fishermen and processing workers are unable to transfer successfully into alternative jobs, they will have to depend upon various types of income transfers for support while unemployed. Although such transfer payments are not technically a "cost" of adjustment, they do represent a redistribution of resources from productive sectors to the unemployed. From the perspective of taxpayers they are seen as an additional financial burden.

Information from interviews reveals that neither fishermen nor processing workers ordinarily meet the income tests for welfare or Medicaid in either Gloucester or New Bedford. This is largely because of the high wages they earn when they are employed. Also, in the case of fishermen from the kinship sector, family resources may be sufficient enough to disqualify them from receiving welfare. A deep and prolonged decline in fishing activity might change this situation, but it is unlikely that the fishing sector will draw upon the system of "safety nets" established for the hard-core poor.

The situation with unemployment insurance, however, is dramatically different. Both fishermen and processing workers regularly rely upon the unemployment insurance system to supplement their incomes during seasonal slumps in fishing activity and during other periods of economic adversity. In this respect, annual earnings from fishing understate the total compensation available to workers attached to the industry.

Although it is difficult to pinpoint quantitatively the patterns of use of unemployment insurance by fishermen and processing workers in New Bedford and Gloucester, there is considerable statewide information on overall utilization of the unemployment insurance system for fishermen

Scallop dredge being repaired in
New Bedford.
Photo: Susan Peterson

and processing workers which is consistent with the findings of the field research. In 1980, for example, over $3 million of unemployment insurance payments were made to commercial fishermen and about another $1 million to workers in the industrial category dominated by processors. In 1981 these amounts were $3.7 million and $2 million respectively. The payments to fishermen represented almost 6 percent of the total wages and salaries covered in that sector, and the payments to processors represented almost 2.5 percent of total covered wages and salaries in this industrial group. This compares to 5.7 percent for construction and an average of .91 percent statewide.

The importance of these numbers is more easily understood in terms of the propensity of various fishing-related industries to utilize the unemployment insurance system. It is well known that seasonal industries, such as construction, rely heavily upon the unemployment insurance system to smooth out fluctuations in earnings caused by weather or shifting patterns of demand. Workers in such industries typically receive more benefits over the course of the year than is paid into the system through payroll taxes. Among these seasonal industries, however, fishing ranked higher than construction in 1980 in the ratio of benefits received to tax payments. The commercial fishing sector received $2.22 in benefits for every payroll tax dollar in 1980, compared to $1.51 for general building contractors and to an average of fifty cents for all firms in the state. Similar results hold for 1981, with fishing receiving $2.44 in benefits compared to $1.66 for contractors and to an average of fifty-nine cents for all firms. Other fishing-related activities such as processing, shipbuilding, and repairing also often rank high by this measure.

It is possible to get a more accurate picture of the importance of unemployment insurance to the annual earnings of fishermen by examining the records of claimants from the sample of unemployed fishermen discussed in chapter 5. Data are available on both annual earnings and annual benefits received for forty-three fishermen in the sample. There are substantial differences between Gloucester and New Bedford fishermen. Consistent with the higher proportion of relatively low earners among the unemployed fishermen in Gloucester, unemployment insurance constitutes a somewhat higher proportion of total income for this group. The median claimant in Gloucester receives between 20 and 30 percent of his annual income from unemployment insurance, and over 60 percent of all claimants receive over 20 percent of their annual income in this way (see table 6–6).[7]

TABLE 6–6   *Distribution of Unemployment Insurance Benefits as a Percent of Annual Earnings for Fishermen, 1981–82*

	Gloucester N = 17	New Bedford N = 23
20% or less	35.3%	69.6%
21–30%	29.4	17.4
31%+	35.3	13.0

SOURCE: Unpublished sample survey, Massachusetts Division of Employment Security

Although it is difficult to predict the exact increase in unemployment as a result of a downturn in the fishing industry, unemployment will rise among both fishermen and fresh-fish processing workers—two groups that already depend disproportionately upon unemployment insurance benefits. Moreover, as the effect of declines in employment and income filter through the local communities, the overall dependence upon unemployment insurance will be further magnified.

Summary

Neither the Gloucester nor New Bedford economy is sufficiently robust to provide an employment cushion for workers displaced from any industry, let alone those from fishing and processing who suffer from severe limitations with respect to marketable skills and education. Gloucester's situation at the time of this study, however, is best understood as a temporary downturn in a previously prosperous economy that has been generally healthy over the past decade and has experienced substantial job growth in manufacturing. Some of these new jobs, such as in metalworking or machining firms, are relatively skilled, but the bulk involve semiskilled assembly or production work. Gloucester's economy is also bolstered by a substantial tourist economy in the summer months.

In contrast, the New Bedford economy has been perennially vulnerable to recessions. Although New Bedford has a broader-based economy in terms of the number of firms and the diversity of industry, many companies are in highly competitive product lines such as apparel, textiles, and shoes, or in segments of the electronics industry, all industries that have been cyclically sensitive. But even before the 1980 recession, New Bedford's economy was considerably weaker than Gloucester's because of its dependence upon declining industries. Moreover, much of its employment base consists of industries where wages are below average for manufacturing.

Although fishing is a smaller proportion of total employment in New Bedford than in Gloucester, it is the main local industry to have been relatively unaffected by recessions. In recent years, fishing and processing have accounted for over one-fifth of the job growth in the New Bedford area, as compared to 14 percent of the job growth in Gloucester.

Over the longer term, if Gloucester can continue expanding in high-growth manufacturing industries, its prospects look somewhat brighter than New Bedford's. In addition, Gloucester's small construction sector is also expected to grow substantially. However, for the short term, it appears that the capacity to absorb the unemployed in both economies will depend on overall improvements in the national economy sufficient not only to provide job growth, but also to reemploy the backlog of workers currently laid off.

Under improved economic conditions, the processing workers and marginal fishermen in New Bedford and Gloucester will have an easier time finding comparable-paying employment in firms such as apparel and light electronic assembly than will the core fishermen. These groups are also likely to be laid off first in the event of an economic downturn. Core fishermen in the kinship sector will face job loss only in downturns that are severe or prolonged.

However, the prospects for the marginal fishermen and processing workers are not uniform in both ports. Given its more robust economy, marginal fishermen in Gloucester are likely to find more stable, high-paying employment, than their counterparts in New Bedford. Processing workers likely to be laid off first in Gloucester, students and part-time adults, should find quite good prospects for reemployment in the seasonal tourist industry. In contrast, in New Bedford, there is no cushion of part-time workers, so when layoffs occur full-time processing workers will be immediately affected. Moreover, in addition to facing a less robust economy many New Bedford processing workers suffer from the twin handicaps of little education and low English proficiency. This restricts their reemployment options largely to the garment industry.

In both Gloucester and New Bedford, the core fishermen will have severe employment problems. They lack transferable skills, beyond the ability to do hard manual labor under arduous physical conditions. Fishing not only provides employment, but employment at high wages that cannot be matched in either community. The most likely prospects are in construction and durable-goods manufacturing. Neither Gloucester nor New Bedford has a prosperous construction industry, particularly involving the higher-paid building trades. Gloucester lacks heavy industry, although it has some relatively well-paid machinist positions, and in New Bedford such industry is on the decline. Thus, if fishermen were to be absorbed, it would only be in unskilled manual jobs or possibly in manufacturing jobs similar to those available to processing workers. Such jobs pay less and are not likely to be the types of work that most fishermen would find acceptable. Thus, core fishermen are likely to undergo a prolonged and difficult adjustment process during which low income, unemployment, and underemployment will persist in the face of a severe downturn in the fishing sector.

These results have especially serious implications for the New Bedford fishermen. The analysis in chapter 5 revealed a substantial capitalist sector in that fishing fleet. Therefore, these fishermen are more likely to find themselves unemployed in a downturn than fishermen protected by the kinship sector, and yet many of these fishermen have strong family and ethnic ties to the New Bedford area. In contrast, many of the fishermen in Gloucester are protected against severe downturns by the kinship labor market. Thus, the economy with the greater absorption difficulties, New Bedford's, is also likely to face the larger unemployment rate among fishermen during a downturn.

The two safety nets available to displaced workers—alternative jobs and unemployment insurance—will both be important. For processing workers, the job safety net is more likely to be a realistic alternative than it is for fishermen. Because of Gloucester's greater prosperity, job alternatives there are more of a possibility than in New Bedford. In both communities, unemployed fishermen will typically have to rely upon unemployment insurance as an alternative to fishing. More generally, both communities will face increased reliance upon unemployment insurance because the loss of fishing jobs and income will affect employment throughout their economies.

SEVEN

Conclusion

The previous chapters have addressed the labor market adjustment process in New England's offshore fishing industry—an industry characterized by small enterprises and diverse institutional arrangements for handling structural change. The picture that emerges is of an industry dependent upon a fluctuating resource that has been subject to a large number of economic shocks over the last few decades. As would be expected, instability in catch, costs, and value has affected jobs and income in the industry, but the patterns of adjustment to change have varied significantly by sector and port.

Traditional analyses, such as employment or income multipliers, provide useful measures of the aggregate impact of economic shocks on regional employment and income, but they cannot reveal the processes by which employment and income adjustments occur. Such analyses are incapable of answering questions like: Which groups of workers in the industry are likely to lose their jobs? Which workers are likely to face reductions in income? What are the employment prospects for displaced workers in each of the cities? In-depth analysis of the fishing and processing labor forces in the two cities reveals the importance of these questions. Underlying the aggregate multipliers are unique institutional characteristics of the employment systems in fishing and processing that shape local adjustment processes.

As has been noted, the presence of significant ethnic groups in both ports—Italians in Gloucester and Portuguese in New Bedford—has resulted in opportunities for new immigrants to enter the industry. These immigrants have augmented the industry's labor supply and have changed its character. They tend to have educational and language disadvantages and they have exceptionally strong attachments to the industry and the local communities.

Italian and Portuguese families have also become increasingly important as owners and operators of vessels. These family-owned vessels give preference to relatives and friends in staffing crew and provide job guarantees not present in other parts of the industry. Moreover, the lay system of compensation in fishing, which is based on income sharing, creates patterns of income variation that are markedly different from pay arrangements tied to the amount of time worked or individual contributions to output. These institutional factors have shaped the ways in which jobs and income are affected by variations in catch and the extent to which resources are transferable to other sectors of the local economy.

Because of ethnic and other institutional distinctions, two types of employment systems can be identified in the fishing industry—kinship and capitalist—each with different implications for adjustment. The kinship system involves job ownership in the form of entitlements for family members to sites on fishing boats. Individuals with strong ethnic and family ties receive income and job guarantees through this system. In contrast, the capitalist systems emphasize efficiency, merit, and seniority in staffing decisions and adjust employment levels to reflect changing levels of output. As a result, the size of the labor force in the capitalist sector can be varied relatively easily and often, while in the kinship sector such variations are highly constrained.

The kinship employment system dominates the fishing sector in Gloucester, but processing is characterized by the capitalist system. In New Bedford, the capitalist system is dominant in both processing and fishing, although the growing Portuguese segment of the finfishing fleet is organized around the kinship system. In both ports there has been a steady expansion of the kinship system in the last two decades and it seems likely that this system will continue to spread throughout the fleets.

Each employment system has different implications for the stability of employment in fishing. The kinship system easily holds labor reserves during an economic downturn, and consequently there is no major short-term bottleneck in securing labor resources during a recovery period. Furthermore, the system is a natural conduit for increasing long-term supplies of labor and capital. Labor can be recruited from abroad through family connections, and considerable financial capital is also readily available by tapping family assets.

This ability to expand easily the employment of experienced and productive crewmen during good times by underemploying these resources in bad times gives the kinship system a competitive edge, which helps explain its growing importance in the industry. The kinship system also creates pressures to maintain boat income and continue growth in order to meet implicit employment and income guarantees. This reinforces the tendency, which is already present due to the common-property nature of the fishing resource, for too many economic resources to flow into the fishing industry.

In the capitalist system there is less pressure for income and growth, but also less ability to hold onto labor during brief downturns. Consequently, adjustment lags during recovery periods are likely to be longer where capitalist systems predominate.

The contrasts between capitalist and kinship employment systems uncovered in this study highlight a larger set of issues involving how economic change is managed in different institutional settings. Economic competition, collective bargaining, and familial institutions all represent alternative arrangements for providing economic security in the face of uncertainty. Market competition, for example, relies heavily upon wage flexibility and the easy transfer of labor from one employer to another with little or no loss in earnings. Almost all studies of labor market adjustment, however, find that there are substantial adjustment costs in the short term, and that displaced workers often face persistent adjustment problems.

Because the competitive market cannot be relied upon to provide economic security, workers often devise other arrangements to bolster their economic position. Under collective bargaining, economic security is often enhanced by preventing wage cuts during economic downturns and by devising various restrictions and penalties to layoffs. Where layoffs cannot be avoided, unions have typically sought to concentrate job loss among the newest workers for whom labor mobility is often easiest, and to negotiate layoff and termination payments. In contrast, kinship and familial solutions to economic insecurity stress job guarantees and the sharing of work and income among family members.

Comparisons with Large-scale Enterprises

Most case studies of adjustment to structural change have focused upon blue-collar workers in medium and large manufacturing firms. These firms generally can be characterized as having capitalist employment systems in which changes in output, or in the staffing requirements of the technology, are translated into changes in employment. Such capitalist systems are also typically associated with relatively rigid, time-based pay systems.

As a result, structural changes that reduce the demand for labor usually result in labor displacement rather than in worksharing or wage flexibility. Either because of seniority provisions in collective bargaining agreements or because of similar practices in nonunion situations, it is the newest workers who usually bear the brunt of the labor redundancy.

Smaller-scale enterprises in the fishing industry exhibit much greater diversity in their institutional mechanisms for dealing with economic change. Some enterprises follow capitalist staffing arrangements and strict seniority, whereas others provide employment guarantees through kinship-based worksharing arrangements. All fishing vessels show considerable wage flexibility through the use of the lay system of pay which ties earnings to the value of catch.

In the case of processing, most enterprises are characterized by the wage rigidity found in large enterprises, but they show more diversity in adjusting their labor supply. Some are more dependent on temporary help hired during peak periods (such as students in the summer), while others prefer to keep a relatively constant year-round work force with flexible work weeks. This diversity is present within the industry in the same port, as well as between ports.

These findings suggest that there are a wider variety of margins for labor market adjustment, and therefore a more complex set of labor market consequences of change, in industries with a major small-business component than in sectors dominated by medium- and large-scale enterprises. Government policies designed to facilitate adjustments to change, improve resource utilization, improve industry performance, or aid local economic development must take these complexities into account.

Implications for Labor Market Adjustment

The most important implication of this study for labor market adjustment is that the institutional features of employment and pay systems in an industry have important consequences both for how adjustment to economic change occurs and for which workers bear the brunt of these adjustments. In addition, the ability and willingness of the work force to migrate and the possession of skills that can be transferred to alternative employment in the local economy are key factors in the adjustment process.

As in most industries, economic downturns in the fishing industry result in job loss among younger and less experienced fishermen. The employment systems in fishing, however, also make those without kinship employment protections more vulnerable to job loss, regardless of age and experience. In processing, seniority with particular employers often determines who suffers job loss during periods of economic decline, but worker productivity may also influence such decisions.

Because the mix between kinship and capitalist adjustments varies by port, the consequences of economic change are unlikely to be uniform in all localities. For example, kinship systems spread income declines from a fall in catch among all workers, whereas capitalist systems concentrate declines on a few workers, who are laid off. Thus, "open" unemployment will be lower in sectors where kinship employment dominates.

This means, on the one hand, that more workers will become unemployed in ports like New Bedford than in ports like Gloucester. On the other hand, the greater importance of job guarantees and income sharing in Gloucester will create disguised unemployment and a decline in per capita earnings, assuming the price of catch remains constant. In fresh-fish processing, a decline in catch will reduce the summer employment of students in some firms in Gloucester, but may reduce the hours of year-round employees in others. In contrast, in New Bedford, where there is very little student employment, adult workers will experience a decline in hours worked and, in some cases, unemployment.

Also contributing to the variation in adjustment problems among ports are the differences in the structure of each port's economy. Industry structure affects the transferability of labor between fishing and other sectors. Neither the Gloucester nor the New Bedford economy provides jobs that will replace the current income of full-time fishermen. However, because the Gloucester economy is generally stronger than that of New Bedford, Gloucester is in a better position to absorb displaced labor. In addition, Gloucester has several high-technology firms with assembly-line jobs offering comparable pay and better conditions than those found in fish processing. Moreover, the seasonal tourist industry in Gloucester is particularly well suited for absorbing young workers who are most likely to be displaced first from processing. In contrast, both the job mix and the overall weakness of the New Bedford economy are likely to make labor adjustment to declines in fishing particularly difficult.

Any movement of labor from fishing to other industries because of a decline in catch is likely to be more difficult in the fishing sector than in the processing sector. Fishing skills, particularly of captains, have led to relatively high incomes for workers with relatively low levels of formal education. Such skills, however, are not transferable to onshore jobs paying comparable wages. Moreover, the strong attachment of many fishermen to their way of life has meant that few fishermen have acquired any work experience outside fishing. In contrast, processing workers are paid at levels more commensurate with other jobs in their localities requiring similar levels of education and skill, and the manual skills in processing have approximate counterparts in semiskilled manufacturing and assembly work.

During a downturn, it is unlikely that much adjustment will take place through the out-migration of fishermen or processing workers from Gloucester or New Bedford. Although workers most likely to be displaced are employed in capitalist rather than kinship systems, many workers in the capitalist system have strong ethnic attachments to their communities, and these ties severely restrict their mobility. In New Bedford, this is compounded by lack of fluency in English among many of these workers. Furthermore, almost all established fishermen have a strong attachment to their industry. Only the young, better-educated, marginal fishermen are likely to view migration as a feasible alternative.

These differences in labor adjustment processes and local economic structure mean that declines in output in the fishing industry will create more visible, and more serious, economic hardships in ports such as New Bedford than in those like Gloucester. Fishermen in New Bedford will experience greater "open" unemployment and declines in processing will reduce the incomes of adult workers more than in Gloucester. At the same time, the employment alternatives for workers in the fishing industry are more limited in New Bedford than in Gloucester. Finally, because the "safety net" of kinship employment systems is less prevalent in New Bedford than in Gloucester, a greater proportion of New Bedford's fishermen will turn to unemployment insurance for economic relief.

Implications for Fisheries Management Policy

There is general agreement in the fisheries literature that, left unmanaged, too many resources will be attracted to the fishing industry. This can lead to depletion of the fishing stock as well as to an inefficient allocation of resources in the economy. As a result, governments manage fishery resources in order to maintain fish populations and prevent over-fishing. Typically, management policies have relied upon controlling fishing methods through gear or area restrictions or upon limiting the effort of the fleet through the use of quotas or licenses. It is generally assumed, however, that if these policies successfully reduce the resources in fishing, these resources will readily be employed elsewhere for more productive purposes.

This focus on controlling fishing effort, to the neglect of the impact of regulation on jobs and income, implicitly assumes perfect mobility of resources into and out of the fishing sector. This study demonstrates that this assumption is often incorrect. Although an initial contraction of the fishing sector will release marginally attached labor, which is likely to be reemployed elsewhere, most fishermen employed in the kinship sector of the industry may be quite immobile for a considerable period of time. These fishermen will probably be underemployed and remain in fishing, rather than be reemployed productively elsewhere.

If the reduction in resources required for efficient management comes from the capitalist sector instead of the kinship sector, fishermen released may also remain unemployed for considerable periods of time. When re-employed, they are also likely to face substantial income loss. Thus, regardless of the type of employment system, contraction will result in underemployed resources, rather than in their productive redeployment to other industrial sectors or other geographic areas.

The immobility of fisheries resources was previously thought to be confined to small, isolated, rural fishing communities.[1] The presence of substantial labor and capital immobility in large fishing ports, involving the core of the industry, is a new finding. Given that there is substantial variation in resource mobility among ports and within a single port, fisheries managers cannot be certain that labor and capital are quite mobile in any fishery, let alone uniformly mobile throughout any particular fishery.

Because resources are likely to be underemployed in fishing during periods of contraction, management plans designed to curtail catch due to overfishing are unlikely to force a more efficient allocation of labor resources when cutbacks extend beyond those marginal vessels and fishermen attached to the capitalist or kinship sector. These findings lend additional support to policies targeted at directly regulating the volume of catch.[2] Current management practices typically involve catch reductions through indirect methods such as size limitations, gear restrictions, and area closures. Economic arguments for direct limitations on catch are reinforced by the increasing importance of the kinship sector and the ease with which resources flow into that sector during industry expansion and the subsequent difficulty in dislodging them during periods of contraction.

Our findings suggest that if current management approaches are continued catch allowances should be more liberal than what would be efficient under an assumption of perfect resource mobility. The immobility of labor, documented in this study, makes it less valuable than if it could be reemployed readily outside the industry.[3]

The research findings also highlight the complementarity between the efficiency objectives of fisheries management policy and local economic development policies. Weak growth and an undiversified industry structure in fishing communities is a major deterrent to surplus labor moving out of the capitalist sector of the fishing industry. If alternative employment prospects for fishing-industry labor are improved in their ports, the opportunity cost to having these resources remain in fishing increases and adjustment flexibility is enhanced. Likewise, management policies designed to restrict catch can have a substantial impact on the overall economic well-being of fishing communities. If declines in jobs and incomes occur as a result of regulatory policy, economic development programs can provide an important buffer. Thus, a comprehensive public policy for the industry should address regulatory questions of entry as well as of catch, and of fishery-industry development as well as resource management.

Our findings are likely to apply to fisheries outside of New England as well as to the specific ports we have studied. The factors that we demonstrate lead to labor immobility are not unique to these ports or to isolated rural ports. Although the dominance of ethnic groups may not always be present, the problems of weak port economies and disadvantaged fishermen are not uncommon in the United States. The types of kinship and family institutions that inhibit labor mobility in Gloucester and New Bedford have also been well documented in developing countries.[4] Whether or not these specific labor market institutions are widespread, however, is far less important than the finding that labor immobility can be a significant problem in large urban ports.

Additional Implications for Local Economic Development Policy

Much of the fishing industry's volatility is beyond the control of local policymakers because it depends on biological occurrences, national demand for fish products, and federal fisheries management policy. However, the fishing industry occupies a unique position in most New England ports because of the number of jobs it provides directly, because of its robust indirect link to local jobs, and because it is the primary source of high-wage employment, particularly for ethnic workers with relatively little education and few alternative skills. The importance of fishing and the lack of economic diversity in many ports further underscore the case for aggressive use of economic development policy to soften the impact of fishing downturns on port economies.

One obvious option is to encourage the development of alternative industries with similar skill and pay characteristics. It is, however, unlikely that any other industry can be found combining the low education requirements of fishing with the relatively high incomes it offers. The primary industry that comes to mind is construction, although it too is notoriously unstable and many of the higher-paying construction jobs require substantial training. Thus, each community will be better off pursuing growth policies that stress economic diversity and an expansion of high-growth industries with substantial low-skill employment, even though this strategy will not provide jobs at comparable earnings to those in fishing.

Another option, often proposed by local industrial development officials, is to strengthen the fishing industry by modernizing piers and other port facilities. Often, however, as is the case in Gloucester and New Bedford, local port improvements are initiated without regard to the long-term prospects of the entire Northwest Atlantic fishing industry. This is a problem because all New England ports rely on a common fishery resource, and so strengthening the industry in one port is likely to be detrimental to other ports. Infrastructure expansion can only be effective if it is coordinated at all levels of government with overall planning for the entire industry, including management policies and international competition.

The connection between growth and institutional adjustment processes must also be considered. Any expansion of port facilities is likely to foster an expansion of the kinship fleet because that sector expands faster than the capitalist fleet. Although the growing dominance of the kinship sector can improve employment stability in both ports, it can also lead to an inefficient and immobile surplus of resources if not closely monitored.

Small Enterprises and Economic Performance

In the case of small enterprises in the fishing industry, the adjustment processes proved more diverse than capitalist arrangements typical of larger-scale enterprises in manufacturing and mining. There is no reason to believe that economic change in other industries dominated by small-scale enterprises would not have similarly complex consequences.

There have been a number of studies, dating back to the early 1970s, on the growth of ethnic enterprises in America.[5] These studies have focused mainly on a small number of ethnic groups—Chinese, Japanese, Koreans, blacks, and Greeks—and describe how ethnic enterprise is fostered through collective responses to the poverty and discrimination of an inhospitable economic environment.

One implication of these studies is that ethnic enterprises and traditional kinship practices represent an alternative to capitalism as a mode of economic organization. In particular, it is a mode that can be highly "competitive" with capitalist economic institutions under certain circumstances.

The literature indicates that ethnic enterprises rely upon *collective* institutions in both labor and capital markets, in contrast to the capitalist model that stresses more *individualistic* forms of organization. There is some indication that these collective arrangements can mobilize capital from relatives and supply it on more favorable terms to ethnic entrepreneurs than those available to their capitalist counterparts without such collective arrangements. In addition, the family and kinship arrangements in the labor market can often motivate effort, loyalty, and flexibility among the work force that are hard to attain under more capitalistic employment relationships.

Whether these "advantages" of ethnic entrepreneurship outweigh the disadvantages of language, foreignness, and discrimination seems to depend on the industry and the product market. For industries that are labor intensive and not subject to significant economies of scale, the kinship model may be highly competitive.

Our findings about the economic performance of kinship vessels in the New England fishing industry support the hypothesis that collective institutions have economic advantages over capitalist institutions. Kinship organizations in fishing have prospered in New England's major ports and are gradually displacing capitalist vessels and collective bargaining institutions. These developments are occurring among well-established ethnic groups and without strong community pressures from new immigration.

Kinship vessels are also likely to have institutional permanence. In addition to providing the kinds of collective organization of capital and labor markets that characterize other types of ethnic enterprises, they are better suited than capitalist institutions to accommodate the volatile and uncertain pattern of catch and price in the fishing industry. Moreover, the relatively high labor earnings provided in fishing and the strong attachment of the work force to fishing as a way of life mean that kinship institutions in fishing are likely to ensure a long-term flow of ethnic labor, capital, and entrepreneurial resources into the industry.

Applications outside the Fishing Industry

Although this book has focused on the fishing industry, its findings and research methodology have much broader application to local and regional policy analysis. It demonstrates a technique for developing detailed economic information and knowledge of processes of economic adjustment by combining readily available statistics with more qualitative field research. The outcome of this analysis is a detailed understanding of the direction and process by which local economic adjustment will occur in response to change in a key local industry. Such understanding is an important aid to local policymakers in identifying key groups likely to be most affected by such change and in directing limited resources in the most effective manner for easing the adjustment process.

This book is more than an assessment of economic change in New England's major fishing ports. It represents a first step in defining the differences in adjustment processes found in industries dominated by small-scale enterprises. In addition, it serves as a general blueprint for local policy research which should be useful to both scholars and practitioners in the field of economic planning and development.

Notes

1. Introduction

1. The case studies conducted prior to the 1960s have been summarized in W. Haber et al., *The Impact of Technological Change: The American Experience* (Kalamazoo, Mich.: W. E. Upjohn Institute for Employment Research, 1963). More recent studies are summarized in J. P. Gordus et al., *Plant Closings and Economic Dislocation* (Kalamazoo, Mich.: W. E. Upjohn Institute for Employment Research, 1981); P. L. Martin, *Labor Displacement and Public Policy* (Lexington, Mass.: D. C. Heath, 1983); and B. Bluestone and B. Harrison, *The Deindustrialization of America* (New York: Basic Books, 1982).

2. See M. Bendick and J. R. Devine, "Workers Dislocated by Economic Change: Do They Need Federal Employment and Training Assistance?" *Seventh Annual Report of the National Commission for Employment Policy* (Washington, D.C.: GPO, 1981), pp. 175–226; L. Jacobson, "Earnings Losses of Workers Displaced from Manufacturing Industries," in *The Impact of International Trade and Investment on Employment,* ed. W. G. Diewald (Washington, D.C.: GPO, 1978); and L. Jacobson, "Earnings Loss Due to Displacement," Working Paper CRC–385 (Arlington, Va.: Public Research Institute of the Center for Naval Analysis, 1979).

3. Gordus et al., *Plant Closings,* p. 92.

4. Depending upon the industry, earnings losses range from a high of 47 percent to a low of 8 percent. See Jacobson, "Earnings Loss Due to Displacement."

5. See S. H. Slichter, E. R. Livernash, and J. J. Healy, *The Impact of Collective Bargaining on Management* (Washington, D.C.: Brookings Institution, 1960), chap. 6.

6. P. B. Doeringer, "Internal Labor Markets and Paternalism in Rural Areas," in *Internal Labor Markets,* ed. P. Osterman (Cambridge: MIT Press, 1984).

7. See J. Tendler, "Ventures in the Informal Sector and How They Worked Out in Brazil," AID Evaluation Special Study no. 12 (Washington, D.C.: U.S. Agency for International Development, March 1983); and G. F. Papanek, H. K. Dey, and D. Wheeler, "Wage Determination in Labor Abundant LDC's: An Alternative Model" (Department of Economics, Boston University, 1984, Mimeographed).

8. See Doeringer, "Internal Labor Markets and Paternalism"; R. P. Dore,

"Commitment—To What, By Whom, and Why," in *Social and Cultural Background of Labor-Management Relations in Asian Countries,* Proceedings of the 1971 Asian Region Conference on Industrial Relations (Tokyo: Japan Institute of Labor, 1971); and R. P. Dore, "The Labour Market and Patterns of Employment in the Wage Sector of LDC's: Implications for the Volume of Employment Generated," *World Development* 2, nos. 4 and 6 (April/May 1974): 1–7.

9. For a more theoretical discussion, see M. J. Piore and C. Sabel, *The Second Industrial Divide* (New York: Basic Books, 1984); and M. Weitzman, *The Share Economy* (Cambridge: MIT Press, 1984).

10. See I. H. Light, *Ethnic Enterprise in America* (Berkeley: University of California Press, 1972); I. H. Light, "Immigrant Entrepreneurs in America: Koreans in Los Angeles," in *Clamor at the Gates: The New American Immigration,* ed. N. Glazer (San Francisco: Institute of Contemporary Studies Press, 1985), pp. 161–78; I. H. Light, "Asian Enterprise in America: Chinese, Japanese, and Koreans in Small Business," in *Self-Help in Urban America: Patterns of Minority Business Enterprise,* ed. S. Cummings (Port Washington, N.Y.: National University Publications, 1980), pp. 33–57; L. A. Lovell-Troy, "Clan Structure and Economic Activity: The Case of Greeks in Small Business Enterprise," in Cummings, *Self-Help,* pp. 58–85; and R. Waldinger, "Immigration and Industrial Change: A Case Study of Immigrants in the New York City Apparel Industry" (Ph.D. diss., Harvard University, 1983).

11. M. Wilkinson, "The Economics of Oceans: Environment, Issues, and Economic Analysis," *American Economic Review, Papers and Proceedings* 69, no. 2 (1979): 251–55.

12. D. Terkla, G. Martini, and A. Sum, "Local Income and Employment Formation" (Institute for Employment Policy, Boston University, 1983, Mimeographed).

13. By focusing on the dominant offshore industry we are neglecting the small-boat, inshore sector. Because the offshore industry is subject to federal resource management policy, data are regularly collected on the industry by the National Marine Fisheries Service. Little data exist on the inshore fishery.

2. New England's Fishing Industry

1. L. J. Smith and S. B. Peterson, "The New England Fishing Industry: A Basis for Management," Technical Report 77–57 (Woods Hole, Mass.: Woods Hole Oceanographic Institution, Aug. 1977), tables 1.4 and 1.5; "U.S. Congress, Senate Committee on Commerce, "Magnuson Fisheries Management and Conservation Act," Report on S.961, 7 Oct. 1975, in *A Legislative History of the Fishery Conservation and Management Act of 1976,* p. 669.

2. U.S. Department of Commerce, National Marine Fisheries Service, *Fishery Statistics of the United States, 1965–1977*, Statistical Digests, nos. 62–70 (Washington, D.C.: GPO, 1968–1983); hereafter cited as *Fishery Statistics*.

3. Ibid.; *Economic Report of the President*, transmitted to Congress, Feb. 1985 (Washington, D.C.: GPO, 1985), table B–1.

4. *Fishery Statistics*, 1965–1976. Because the statistics do not distinguish between the catches of offshore and inshore vessels, all figures for groundfish landings and the value of the catch include the inshore fishery.

5. *Fishery Statistics*, 1965–1976; S. Clark, "Current Status of the Georges Bank (5Ze) Haddock Stock," International Commission for the Northwest Atlantic Research Document no. 75/48, June 1975; New England Regional Fishery Management Council, "Atlantic Groundfish," supplement no. 2 to Final Environmental Impact Statement, draft, May 1978, p. 9.

6. *Fishery Statistics*, 1965–1976.

7. U.S. Congress, House of Representatives, *Fisheries Promotion: Hearings before Committee on Merchant Marine and Fisheries*, 93d Cong., 2d sess., 11 June 1974, p. 874; "Fishermen Tell What They Think of Their Industry," *Gloucester Daily Times*, 26 June 1970.

8. J. Enos, " '74 Was Good to Gloucester Despite Inflation, Less Fish," *National Fisherman* 55, no. 13 (1975): 71; B. Cahill, "Fishermen in Trouble? 'Hogwash'," *Gloucester Daily Times*, 13 March 1975; U.S. Bureau of the Census, *Statistical Abstract of the United States: 1978* (Washington, D.C.: GPO, 1978), table no. 695.

9. R. L. Corey and J. B. Dirlam, "Current Developments in Ex-Vessel Groundfish Prices," Marine Memorandum 65 (Kingston: University of Rhode Island, Nov. 1981), table 12; *Economic Report of the President*, 1985, table B–1.

10. ICNAF, "List of Fishing Vessels and Summary of Fishing Effort in the ICNAF Convention Area, 1965" (Dartmouth, Nova Scotia: ICNAF, 1967); ICNAF, "List of Fishing Vessels, 1974" (Dartmouth, Nova Scotia: ICNAF, 1976); P. V. Mulkern, "Annual Earnings of Boston Fishermen in 1964," Regional Report (Boston: Bureau of Labor Statistics, Feb. 1966); J. Ackert, Gorton Corporation, Gloucester, Mass., personal communication, spring 1978.

11. See chapter 4; *Fishery Statistics*, 1965–1969.

12. *Fishery Statistics*, 1965–1976; New England Fishery Management Council, "Fishery Management Plan, Final Environmental Impact Statement, Regulatory Impact Review for Atlantic Sea Scallops (*Placopecten magellanicus*)" (Saugus, Mass.: New England Fishery Management Council, Jan. 1982), pp. 33–38.

13. U.S. Department of Commerce, National Marine Fisheries Service, *Scallops 1930–72, Basic Economic Indicators*, Current Fisheries Statistics no. 6127

(Washington, D.C.: U.S. Department of Commerce, June 1973), p. 2; U.S. Department of Commerce, *Historical Statistics of the United States* (Washington, D.C.: GPO, 1975), ser. D740; New England Fishery Management Council, "Draft Sea Scallop Fishery Management Plan for the Northwest Atlantic, Part 1—Statement of the Problem" (Peabody, Mass.: New England Fishery Management Council, July 1979), p. 14; *Economic Report of the President,* table B–1.

14. M. A. Altobello, D. A. Storey, and J. M. Conrad, "The Atlantic Sea Scallop Fishery: A Descriptive and Econometric Analysis," Massachusetts Agricultural Experiment Station, Research Bulletin no. 643 (Amherst: University of Massachusetts, Jan. 1977), p. 14, table 4.2; New England Fishery Management Council, "Fishery Management Plan . . . for Scallops," pp. 36, 39; ICNAF, "List, 1965"; ICNAF, "List of Fishing Vessels, 1971 with Summaries of Fishing Effort for 1969, 1970, and 1971" (Dartmouth, Nova Scotia: ICNAF, 1972); E. Lardner, "New Bedford Scalloper to Help Develop New Alaska Fishery," *National Fisherman* 48, no. 12 (1968): 13B; R. Bouchard, "Three More Scallopers Heading West for Alaska," ibid. 49, no. 2 (1968): 3A; T. V. McCarthy, "New Bedford Fishermen Demand Import Duty on Canadian Scallops," ibid. 54, no. 4 (1973): 3A; D. A. Storey and C. E. Willis, "Econometric Analysis of Atlantic Sea Scallop Markets," submitted to New England Regional Fishery Management Council, Feb. 1978, fig. 2.7; H. H. Harp, "The Food Marketing Cost Index: A New Measure for Analyzing Food Price Changes," U.S. Department of Agriculture, National Economics Division, Technical Bulletin no. 1633 (Washington, D.C.: Economics, Statistics, and Cooperatives Service, Aug. 1980), table 4; *Economic Report of the President,* table B–24.

15. New England Fishery Management Council, "Draft Sea Scallop Management Plan," p. 14; New England Fishery Management Council, "Fishery Management Plan . . . for Scallops," p. 39; U.S. Department of Commerce, National Marine Fisheries Service, *Massachusetts Landings, 1976; Fishery Statistics, 1976.*

16. Altobello, Storey, and Conrad, "Atlantic Sea Scallop Fishery," pp. 36–40; see chapter 4.

17. M. E. Dewar, *Industry in Trouble: The Federal Government and the New England Fisheries* (Philadelphia: Temple University Press, 1983), pp. 15–19.

18. D. Arnold and J. Lanzillo, "Massachusetts Inshore Draggermen's Association—Cape Cod Commercial Fishermen's Coalition Plan," Jan. 1978, tables following p. 4; U.S. Congress, House of Representatives, *Fishery Jurisdiction: Hearings before Committee on Merchant Marine and Fisheries,* 93d Cong., 2d sess., May–October 1974, pp. 71, 100.

19. *Fishery Statistics,* 1976 and 1977; New England Fishery Management Council, "Interim Fishery Management Plan for Atlantic Groundfish" (Saugus,

Mass.: New England Fishery Management Council, Sept. 30, 1981), p. 32; Discussions at meetings of the New England Fishery Management Council, 1977; Bureau of the Census, *Statistical Abstract,* 1979, p. 425.

20. *Fishery Statistics,* 1976 and 1977; J. Jessen and M. E. Smith, anthropologists working in New Bedford, personal communication; Bureau of the Census, *Statistical Abstract,* 1979, p. 425.

21. M. Dewar, R. Lake, M. Lord, D. Wishner, and J. Wondolleck, "The Fishing Industry of Chatham and Its Importance to the Town" (Department of Urban Studies and Planning, Massachusetts Institute of Technology, Aug. 1978), p. 24.

22. J. Laitin, "Boston Fish Pier Renovation Draws Mixed Reaction," *National Fisherman* 62, no. 8 (1981): 2–3; J. Sperling, "Portland, Maine, Fishermen Wary about Harbor Development Plans," ibid. 63, no. 2 (1982): 20–21; H. V. R. Palmer, "Cape Cod Expands Harbor Facilities for Fishermen," ibid. 62, no. 2 (1981), 20–22.

23. Public Law 94–265, Fishery Conservation and Management Act of 1976.

24. Although yellowtail flounder is not a groundfish, the New England Fishery Management Council included it in the groundfish management plan in order to restrict fishing as soon as the law went into effect.

25. Dewar, *Industry in Trouble,* pp. 154–72. The discussion of management that follows also relies on this source.

26. L. Stevens, "Haddock Problems Presented Forcefully," *Commercial Fisheries News,* Dec. 1982, p. 14; "Yellowtail Survey Shows Stock Improving," ibid., May 1983, p. 24.

27. Public Law 94–265, sec. 303.

28. National Marine Fisheries Service, unpublished data, 1980–1982; New England Fishery Management Council, "Interim Fishery Management Plan," p. 32.

29. N. Mencher, "Soaring Fuel Costs Sap Slim Profits from Low-Priced Fish," *Gloucester Daily Times,* 6 June 1980; P. Garcia, "400 New Bedford Fishermen Refuse to Fish," *Boston Globe,* 29 May 1980; B. O'Donnell, "Sliding Prices Alarm Fishermen," *Gloucester Daily Times,* 14 May 1981.

30. New England Fishery Management Council, "Interim Fishery Management Plan," p. 19; B. O'Donnell, "Fish Boom Peaks: Riding Through the Economic Valley," *Gloucester Daily Times,* 5 Sept. 1981.

31. T. Sullivan, "Old Boats May Prevail As Fuel Cost Squeeze Tightens," *National Fisherman* 61, no. 12 (1981), p. 2.

32. New England Fishery Management Council, "Fishery Management Plan . . . for Scallops," part 8.

33. Ibid.

34. *Fishery Statistics,* 1977; National Marine Fisheries Service, unpublished data, 1978–1982.

35. New England Fishery Management Council, "Fishery Management Plan . . . for Scallops," p. 66.

36. Ibid., p. 39.

37. S. Peterson and L. J. Smith, "Small-Scale Commercial Fishing in Southern New England," Technical Report 81–72 (Woods Hole, Mass.: Woods Hole Oceanographic Institution, Aug. 1981), p. 31.

3. The Structure of the Fishing Industry in Gloucester and New Bedford

1. Economic Research Associates, "Information for a Development Plan for Gloucester's Inner Harbor," September 1980; and J. Kelley, F. Rubin, and C. Newick, *The New England Fleet: 1980 Inventory* (Durham: Complex Systems Research Center, University of New Hampshire, June 1983).

The processing figure is for 1979 and is in terms of weight of processed groundfish. The figure represents the percent of processing in Massachusetts accounted for by Gloucester and New Bedford processors as almost all processing of groundfish in New England is done in Massachusetts. See D. Georgiana and R. Ibara, "Groundfish Processing in Massachusetts During the 1970's," *Marine Fisheries Review,* January 1983.

2. The following historical material draws from D. J. White, *The New England Fishing Industry* (Cambridge: Harvard University Press, 1954); and two manuscripts by S. Peterson, R. Pollnac, and J. Poggie, "The Fisherman of Southern New England: A Social Cultural Survey" and "The New Bedford Fishery." They, in turn, draw primarily from J. B. Connolly, *The Port of Gloucester* (New York: Doubleday, Doran and Co., 1940); H. Haberland, "Gloucester— Three Centuries a Fishing Port," *Commercial Fisheries Review* 8 (1946): 1–5; F. Mitchell, "The Decline of Whaling in New Bedford 1857 to 1875" (M.A. thesis, University of Rhode Island, 1971); and S. L. Wolfbein, *The Decline of a Cotton Textile City: A Study of New Bedford* (New York: AMS Press, 1968).

3. These figures are based on data maintained by the National Marine Fisheries Service and have been provided by Susan Peterson. The figures refer to port of landing, not port of registration, and are based on frequency of appearance, not on poundage landed. Five gross tons is the smallest vessel for which federal statistics are collected.

4. These figures and those in the following paragraph are based on data provided to us by the National Marine Fisheries Service.

5. Employment figures, based upon data from the Massachusetts Division of Employment Security, report only "covered employment" and therefore understate total employment.

6. Some evidence on the seasonality of fishing is available from unpublished data provided to us by the Massachusetts Division of Employment Security. This information, from ES–202 forms, contains quarterly employment data on boats that are covered by unemployment insurance. For the four quarters of 1980, the employment in fishing in New Bedford was 1,833 for the first quarter, 2,017 for the second, 2,191 for the third, and 2,064 for the fourth. For employment in processing, the numbers were, respectively, 1,054, 1,248, 1,213, and 1,131. Clearly there is a drop-off in the winter.

7. The figure of sixty gross registered tons as a breakpoint between small and large boats is, of course, arbitrary, but this figure is conventionally used in fishery statistics.

8. White, *New England Fishing Industry,* pp. 86–88.

9. Recently, high debt burdens have been compounded by large increases in vessel insurance rates, which resulted from a rash of recent sinkings of Gloucester fishing boats. Since 1980 thirty-six Gloucester fishing boats worth a total of almost $11 million have sunk, compared to only fourteen sinkings of New Bedford boats. There is no factual evidence, as of yet, that any of these sinkings were intentional. Twenty-three of the Gloucester vessels were offshore draggers and over 80 percent of these were more than twenty years old, many with second mortgages. The fishing industry claims recent reductions in catch have resulted in fishermen delaying needed maintenance which increases the probability of sinking. If some of these sinkings were intentional, this supports the view that transferring capital out of the industry is very difficult. Moreover, there is some evidence that many of the fishermen whose vessels sunk are not leaving the industry, but either own other boats or are in the process of purchasing new vessels.

10. Kelley, Rubin, Newick, *The New England Fleet.*

11. White, *New England Fishing Industry,* pp. 42–56.

12. Ibid., pp. 57–101.

4. Fishermen, Processing Workers, and Their Jobs

1. The basis for this chapter is unpublished data from 1972 through 1981 collected by Susan Peterson and Richard Pollnac as well as the following published reports: S. Peterson and L. J. Smith, "Small-Scale Commercial Fishing in Southern New England," Technical Report 81–72 (Woods Hole, Mass.: Woods Hole Oceanographic Institution, Aug. 1981); S. Peterson and L. J. Smith, "New England Fishing, Processing and Distribution," Technical Report 79–52 (Woods Hole, Mass.: Woods Hole Oceanographic Institution, 1979); J. Poggie and C. Gersuny, *Fishermen of Galilee,* Marine Bulletin Series no. 17 (Kingston: University of Rhode Island, 1974); R. Pollnac, "Continuity and Change in Marine Fishing Communities," Anthropology

Working Paper no. 10 (Kingston: University of Rhode Island, 1976); R. Pollnac and J. Poggie, "Sociocultural Variables Related to Variance in Perception of Alternative Fishing Types in Southern New England," Anthropology Working Paper no. 27 (Kingston: University of Rhode Island, 1978); M. Miller and R. Pollnac, "Responses to the Fisheries Conservation and Management Act of 1976: The Port of Gloucester" (University of Rhode Island, 1978, Mimeographed); R. Pollnac, S. Peterson, and J. Poggie, "The Fishermen of Southern New England: A Sociocultural Overview," Report to the U.S. Department of State, June 1982; L. J. Smith and S. B. Peterson, "The New England Fishing Industry: A Basis for Management," Technical Report 77–57 (Woods Hole, Mass.: Woods Hole Oceanographic Institution, 1977).

2. A *Labor Market Area* (LMA) encompasses a central city or cities and the surrounding territory within commuting distance. It is "an economically integrated geographical unit within which workers may readily change jobs without changing their place of residence."

3. Unpublished survey by Susan Peterson.

4. These high earnings can be thought of as intramarginal rents or a "producer surplus"—income above their opportunity costs. This surplus is important because often it is not transferable to other occupations if these fishermen are forced out of fishing. See P. Copes, "Factor Rents, Sole Ownership and the Optimum Level of Fisheries Exploitation," *Manchester School of Economic and Social Studies* 40, no. 2 (1972): 145–63.

5. U.S. Census of Population, 1980; Public Use Sample.

6. J. B. Connolly, *The Port of Gloucester* (New York: Doubleday, Doran and Co., 1940).

7. Miller and Pollnac, "Responses to the Fisheries Conservation and Management Act of 1976," p. 93.

8. Pollnac and Poggie, "Sociocultural Variables."

9. Pollnac, Peterson, and Poggie, "The Fishermen of Southern New England."

10. Ibid., Annex 4, p. 22.

11. Pollnac and Poggie, "Sociocultural Variables."

12. For example, see J. Aronoff, *Psychological Needs and Cultural Systems* (Princeton: C. Van Nostrand, 1967); B. McCay, "Optimal Foragers or Political Actors? Ecological Analysis of a New Jersey Fishery," *American Ethnologist* 8 (1981): 356–82; B. McCay, "Systems Ecology, People Ecology, and the Anthropology of Fishing Communities," *Human Ecology* 6 (1978): 397–422; M. Orbach, *Hunters, Seamen and Entrepreneurs* (Berkeley: University of California Press, 1977); Pollnac, "Continuity and Change in Marine Fishing Communities"; Pollnac and Poggie, "Sociocultural Variables."

13. M. Orbach, "Social and Cultural Aspects of Limited Entry," in *Limited*

Entry as a Fishery Management Tool, ed. R. B. Rettig and J. C. Ginter (Seattle: University of Washington Press, 1978), pp. 211–29.

14. Poggie and Gersuny, *Fishermen of Galilee,* p. 6.

15. Pollnac and Poggie, "Sociocultural Variables."

16. Peterson and Smith, "Small-Scale Commercial Fishing in Southern New England"; Pollnac and Poggie, "Sociocultural Variables."

17. Pollnac, Peterson, and Poggie, "The Fishermen of Southern New England," p. 10.

18. F. Danowski, *Fishermen's Wives: Coping with an Extraordinary Occupation,* Marine Bulletin no. 37 (Kingston: University of Rhode Island, 1980), p. 18.

19. Ibid., p. 20.

20. Orbach, *Hunters, Seamen and Entrepreneurs;* R. Andersen, "Hunt and Deceive: Information Management in Newfoundland Deep-Sea Trawler Fishing," in *North Atlantic Fishermen,* ed. R. Andersen and C. Wadel (St. Johns: Memorial University of Newfoundland, 1972), pp. 120–40; J. Tunstall, *The Fishermen* (London: MacGibbon and Kee, 1962).

21. Danowski, *Fishermen's Wives.*

22. Smith and Peterson, "The New England Fishing Industry."

23. Pollnac, Peterson, and Poggie, "The Fishermen of Southern New England," Annex 4, p. 22.

24. Peterson and Smith, "New England Fishing, Processing and Distribution"; D. Georgianna, P. Greenwood, R. Ibara, and R. Ward, "A Method of Estimating Fish Processing Capacity in Massachusetts and New Hampshire" (North Dartmouth, Mass.: Southeastern Massachusetts University Foundation, College of Business and Industry, 1977).

5. Labor Market Structure and Labor Force Adjustment

1. S. Peterson and L. J. Smith, "Small-Scale Commercial Fishing in Southern New England," Technical Report 81–72 (Woods Hole, Mass.: Woods Hole Oceanographic Institution, Aug. 1981), p. 8.

2. Ibid., pp. 18–28.

3. Ibid., pp. 10–14.

4. See M. L. Miller and J. Van Maanen, "Boats Don't Fish, People Do: Ethnographic Notes on the Federal Management of Fisheries," *Human Organization* 38, no. 4 (1979): 377–85.

5. For a discussion of the lay system, see A. A. Holmsen, "Remuneration, Ownership and Investment Decisions in the Fishing Industry," Marine Technical Report no. 1 (Kingston: University of Rhode Island, January 1972, Mimeographed); and J. G. Sutinen, "Fishermen's Remuneration Systems and

Implications For Fisheries Development," *Scottish Journal of Political Economy* 26, no. 2 (1979): 147–62.

6. To provide some sense of the magnitudes involved, a typical lay system on a New Bedford dragger divides the catch revenue in the following way: (1) 4.5 percent of the total catch revenue is paid to the fishermen's union; (2) boat overhead and operating costs are then deducted; (3) the balance is divided 48 percent for the boat owner and 52 percent for the crew. Food expenses are then deducted from the crew's portion and the remaining money is divided among the crew in equal shares. The boat owner pays the captain a bonus (usually equal to one crew share) and retains the remainder of the vessel share (see Holmsen, "Remuneration, Ownership and Investment Decisions").

7. See D. J. White, *The New England Fishing Industry* (Cambridge: Harvard University Press, 1954); and Sutinen, "Fishermen's Remuneration Systems."

8. See White, *New England Fishing Industry*.

9. Holmsen, "Remuneration, Ownership and Investment Decisions"; and Sutinen, "Fishermen's Remuneration Systems."

10. See White, *New England Fishing Industry;* and M. E. Dewar, *Industry in Trouble: The Federal Government and the New England Fisheries* (Philadelphia: Temple University Press, 1983).

11. For an attempt at quantifying these effects, see P. B. Doeringer, P. I. Moss, and D. G. Terkla, "Capitalism and Kinship: Do Institutions Matter in the Labor Market?" *Industrial and Labor Relations Review* 40, no. 1 (1986).

12. For a detailed discussion of the importance of the Atlantic Fishermen's Union during the "pre-kinship" period in Gloucester see White, *New England Fishing Industry*.

13. The data reported are derived from a 10 percent sample of unemployed workers previously employed as fishermen who registered for unemployment benefits in Massachusetts between October 1981 and March 1982. The sample contains 133 of the unemployed fishermen in Massachusetts, including 69 from New Bedford and 43 from Gloucester. Because the sample covers only those with sufficient prior work experience to be eligible for unemployment insurance, this group can be presumed to have a reasonable degree of attachment to fishing. The most casual fishermen who had worked less than fifteen weeks during the previous year or who had earned less than $1,200 in the previous three months are excluded. The cause of unemployment, whether due to economic conditions or vessel repairs, for example, could not be determined.

6. Employment and Income Alternatives to Fishing and Processing

1. The data in this, and the following two paragraphs, are derived from U.S. Department of Commerce, *General Social and Economic Charac-*

teristics—Massachusetts, 1980 Census of Population, PC80–1–C–23, Issued
June 1983.

2. These data were collected by the Massachusetts Division of Employment
Security (DES) and only include employment in establishments subject to state
employment-security laws. Essentially, these statistics exclude government
employment and the self-employed as well as some small firms. In addition, the
DES data refer to the New Bedford and Gloucester Labor Market Areas (LMAs) as
opposed to the Standard Metropolitan Statistical Area (SMSA) or city. In the
case of New Bedford, the LMA is the same as the SMSA except for the exclusion
of one small nearby city.

Extension of the state employment-security laws resulted in coverage of state
and local governments in 1978. To maintain a consistent data base throughout the 1970–80 period, only private sector employment has been included.
Standard industrial code (SIC) 19, ordinance work, was discontinued in 1974 as
a separate category and merged with the industries in SIC 34—fabricated metal
products. For consistency, employment in SIC 19 has been included with
SIC 34 for 1970 through 1973 as well. In addition, nonprofit organizations such
as state hospitals, colleges, and universities were included in the "services"
category in 1972, thus lending an upward bias to the 1970–1975 employment
changes reported for each city.

For additional information on the DES data, see Massachusetts Division of
Employment Security, *Annual Planning Information Report, Fiscal Year 1982,
Massachusetts* (Boston: Commonwealth of Massachusetts, 1982).

3. Ibid.

4. G. Masnick and J. Pitkin, *The Changing Population of States and Regions:
Analysis and Projections* (Boston: Joint Center of Urban Studies of MIT and
Harvard University, 1982).

5. In Gloucester, most of the employment growth over the next decade is
expected in manufacturing, trade, and construction. Construction employment
is expected to increase 50 percent, but construction represents only a little more
than 3 percent of Gloucester's current employment. Both manufacturing and
trade employment are projected to increase by around 30 percent. However, the
manufacturing projection is based almost totally on expansion in high technology, a sector that is subject to future uncertainty. The projected increase in
retail trade employment is concentrated in the eating and drinking industry
(SIC 581), a traditionally strong sector in Gloucester.

In New Bedford, area projections are not available. However, employment
projections for the southeastern Massachusetts region indicate 18 to 20 percent
reductions in the apparel industry with 15 to 20 percent increases in the finance,
insurance and real estate, retail trade, and services sectors. Construction employment is expected to increase by over 30 percent. New Bedford currently
accounts for over 35 percent of the total southeastern Massachusetts employ-

ment in the nondurable goods sector, but it accounts for only about 15 percent of total southeastern Massachusetts employment in each of the sectors that are expected to grow. For additional information, see P. Harrington, "Industry Employment Projections for the Gloucester Labor Market Area, 1980–1990" (Center for Labor Market Studies, Northeastern University, 1983) and Massachusetts Division of Employment Security, "Southeast Region Employment: Projected Changes, 1980–1990" (Boston: Commonwealth of Massachusetts, 1983).

6. For an analysis of labor markets in the "high-technology" sector, see P. B. Doeringer and P. Pannell, "Manpower Strategies for New England's High Technology Sector," in *New England's Vital Resources: The Labor Force*, ed. J. C. Hoy and M. H. Bernstein (Washington, D.C.: American Council on Education, 1982), pp. 11–35.

7. These figures are subject to two caveats. First, they only apply to "covered employment," employment in establishments large enough to be eligible for participation in the unemployment insurance system. For fishing this excludes all vessels of less than ten tons. As a result, fishermen on smaller boats are denied any benefits from the system. Second, the payroll data include all fishermen on boats over ten tons, whether they worked one day or all year. Eligibility for unemployment insurance, however, requires that a fisherman be employed for at least fifteen weeks. Because some fishermen work for only part of the year, usually in the summer, the earnings supplement received by fishermen with enough attachment to the industry to be eligible for unemployment insurance is higher than the benefit data would suggest.

7. Conclusion

1. See, for example, L. G. Anderson, *The Economics of Fisheries Management* (Baltimore: Johns Hopkins University Press, 1977); F. W. Bell, *Food from the Sea: The Economics and Politics of Ocean Fisheries* (Boulder, Colo.: Westview Press, 1978); J. A. Crutchfield, "Economic and Social Implications of the Main Policy Alternatives for Controlling Fishing Effort," *Journal of the Fisheries Reserve Board of Canada* 36 (1979): 742–52.

2. Often mentioned policies for directly regulating the volume of catch are limiting entry of vessels or fishermen, or individual transferable quotas. Limiting vessels, however, may lead to inefficiencies because there are incentives for fishermen to add equipment and labor to licensed vessels in order to increase catch. An analogous problem results if labor alone is limited. Individual quotas assign a specific amount of allowable catch to each fisherman. These should be transferable so that fishermen can sell their unused quotas or purchase additional quotas. This ensures that the most cost-efficient fishermen will receive the

largest quotas. Individual quotas, however, also have some drawbacks. They involve very high enforcement costs and, in the presence of heterogeneous productivity among the fishermen, can be inefficient. There has been much discussion of these two alternatives in the literature—see Crutchfield, "Economic and Social Implications"; Bell, *Food from the Sea;* Anderson, *Economics of Fisheries Management;* P. H. Pearse, "Fishing Rights, Regulations, and Revenue, *Marine Policy* 5, no. 2 (1981): 135–46; and R. N. Johnson and G. D. Libecap, "Contracting Problems and Regulations: The Case of the Fishery," *American Economic Review* 72, no. 5 (1982): 1005–22.

3. For a more detailed discussion of this see D. Terkla, P. Doeringer, and P. Moss, "Widespread Labor Stickiness in the New England Offshore Fishing Industry: Implications for Adjustment and Regulation" (Boston University, Department of Economics Discussion Paper, 1986).

4. P. Alexander, "Do Fisheries Experts Aid Fisheries Development: The Case of Sri Lanka," *Maritime Studies and Management* 3, no. 1 (1975): 5–11; O. Brox, *Newfoundland Fishermen in the Age of Industry: A Sociological Study of Economic Dualism,* Newfoundland Social and Economic Studies, no. 9 (Toronto: University of Toronto Press, 1972); T. M. Fraser, *Fishermen of Southern Thailand* (New York: Holt, Rinehart, and Winston, 1966); M. Sahidin, "Pakistan: Management of Fisheries Resources," in *Man, Land, and Sea,* ed. C. Soysa, L. S. Chia, and W. L. Collier (Bangkok: The Agricultural Development Council, 1982), pp. 199–218.

5. For a review of these studies, see S. Cummings, *Self-Help in Urban America: Patterns of Minority Business Enterprise* (Port Washington, N.Y.: National University Publications, 1980); R. Waldinger, "Immigration and Industrial Change: A Case Study of Immigrants in the New York City Apparel Industry" (Ph.D. diss., Harvard University, 1983).

Index